In the Spirit of Armorbearing

In the Spirit of Armorbearing

✦

Being the Gift of Support to God's Leaders

Earma Broadway Brown

Writers Club Press

San Jose New York Lincoln Shanghai

In the Spirit of Armorbearing
Being the Gift of Support to God's Leaders

Writers Club Press
an imprint of iUniverse, Inc.

For information address:
iUniverse, Inc.
5220 S. 16th St., Suite 200
Lincoln, NE 68512
www.iuniverse.com

Unless otherwise indicated, all Scripture quotations are taken from the Holy Bible: New International Version, Copyright © 1983 by the B.B. Kirkbridge Bible Company, Inc. and The Zondervan Corporation, Grand Rapids, Michigan.

Verses marked TLB are taken from The Living Bible, © 1971 by Tyndale House Publishers.
Verses marked AMP are taken from The Amplified Bible, © 1965 by Zondervan Publishing House.
Verses marked KJV are taken from the King James Version Bible, © 2000 by The Zondervan Corporation.

Editorial Consultants: Andria Ayers, Marilyn Worsham

ISBN: 0-595-25095-5 (pbk)
ISBN: 0-595-65035-X (cloth)

Printed in the United States of America

This book is dedicated to my sweetheart Varn, who exemplifies a modern-day armorbearer. Varn, I have often marveled at your devotion and dedication to our leader. I believe our Lord has been pleased, too. Thank you for your example. More than that thank you for your support and affirmation of me as a woman of God. We are co-laborers in Christ.

I myself have selected your fellow Levites from among the Israelites as a gift to you, dedicated to the Lord to take care of the details at the Tent of Meeting.
—Numbers 18:6 New International Version Bible

Contents

PREFACE

A ministry leader's job can be one of the loneliest in the world. Our ministry leaders are the ones to whom many people turn with their problems. Yet, when they need encouragement and support they sometimes find no one. When the pastor has cared for the last sheep of the day, or the evangelist has prayed for his last convert, who is there to understand their unique need? God did not intend it to be this way. In Old Testament days, He designed a beautiful chain of support. He literally called out the Levites, specifically as a support ministry and gave it to His leadership team as a gift.[1] God's design and gift is still active today through the helps ministry. [2]

I have written this book as a teaching tool. I seek to bring clarity and fresh insight on serving as armorbearers through this ministry gift of helps. Furthermore, I hope to rally God's people to share in a stronger support of His authorities in His Church. Whether you are a leader who needs your support team to have a greater revelation of their place, a seasoned minister of helps or a layman God has called from the pew to help hold up the arms of your leadership, there is something for each of us in this study. I anticipate whatever level of authority you serve Christ; you will be enriched by applying these principles.

The study has been divided into two parts. Part one addresses the spirit of armorbearing that can be applied to any administration of the helps ministry. Part two directs its attention to one called by God to be an armorbearer to a specific leader. Throughout the chapters, I introduce or examine an aspect of this ministry of assistance called armorbearing. In the *Pattern Your Service* portion of each chapter, I offer examples by which we can pattern our service. *Things Worth Remembering* was written to concisely bring out ministry of helps principles that will stick with us. Recognizing the need for the development of our gift to serve, the *Gift Cultivated* section was birthed. I offer practical application for these principles through the *Daily Life* section of each chapter. Finally, queries designed to spur action are presented at the end of each chapter.

My prayer is that our Father God will use this study to further impart the spirit of armorbearing to the Body of Christ. Also, I pray that He may empower His servants to greater faithfulness and honor. There is a need for more people to take up this worthy calling and commit to do whatever it takes to support their Church's leadership. Too many of our leaders have struggled long enough, individually holding out the staff of God over the battle of faith. I believe some have fallen, not because they lacked an anointing, but because they lacked the supporters that understood the times or their place in ministry.[3] As each God-appointed helper takes his place, I know within my spirit that specialized plans of the enemy for our leaders' demise in the Body of Christ will be stopped, scattered and become null and void. Now is the time for those called to operate in the spirit of armorbearing to assume their position holding up the arms of God's leaders. This book was birthed out of a desire to see others walk in the fullness of their calling to serve Christ through serving others.

Perhaps you have been looking for this servant's path of ministry in your life or local church. My hope is that you find this book to be a useful guideline for the path God has called you as an armorbearer. I see more men and women obtaining a fresh perspective of their service being a God-ordained ministry. I see more laymen entering their place of service as helpers and armorbearers to God's carriers of the gospel. I envision more leaders being refreshed and obtaining fresh vision because they are helped by others walking in their place of service and support. Come walk with me and examine the spirit of armorbearing.

Earma Broadway Brown

ACKNOWLEDGEMENTS

My deepest thanks to those who have contributed to my life and this book:

My *Heavenly Father,* thank You for entrusting me with Your ministry. May it bring much fruit to Your glory.

My Pastors *Mike and Kathy Hayes,* you have held out a shining example of excellence in life to me; I am always challenged to excel when I am around you two. Thank you.

Chief Armorbearer *Susan Thomas* along with *Charlotte and Kenneth Tasby,* thank you for being living epistles. I acknowledge you captured the spirit and heart of armorbearing long before I decided to write a book. You have imparted to me the spirit of armorbearing and often spurred me to a spirit of excellence.

PART I
OPERATING IN THE SPIRIT OF ARMORBEARING

1

WHAT IS AN ARMORBEARER?

○ ○

Saul liked him very much and David became one of his armorbearers.

——*1 Samuel 16:22b*

In biblical days, an armorbearer was one who actually carried the shield and armor of his leader as he went into battle, often acting as his personal assistant. For example, King Saul had several armorbearers assigned to him.[1] In our modern-day, I see no one walking around fully suited in the classical armor of the early centuries. Nevertheless, in the spiritual realm, we continue to need our armor. The Ephesians' writer commands us to put on the full armor of God so that we can take our stand against the devil's schemes.[2] Just as much as our early century counterparts, we in the ministry of service are to suit up in the Armor of the Spirit and carry the armor of God's leaders in the battle of faith.

The term "armorbearer" was originally translated from the Hebrew word, *nasa*, meaning to figuratively or literally lift up, support or simply help.[3] On occasion, Bible translators have translated the word, "help", from the Hebrew word, *nasa*. In light of these defining terms, we can see an armorbearer is one that helps or supports the arms of an assigned leader during the times of battle.

A modern day armorbearer is one called by God to serve and help his assigned leader in life, ministry, and especially in the fight of faith.[4] In essence, an armorbearer is called to attend to, minister to, care for, help, be of use, assist, benefit, promote, support, make easy for, nourish, and encourage their leader.

Furthermore, God calls others to walk in the spirit of armorbearing. They may not be assigned specifically to one leader, but they possess the mindset and attitude of an armorbearer. The attitude of an armorbearer is one of servanthood. The mindset of an armorbearer, as well as those operating in the spirit of one, is to do what it takes to serve and support their leadership.[5] Operating in the spirit of armorbearing can also be described as operating in the principles or pervading qualities of an armorbearer. The qualities that top the list are servanthood, commitment, attentiveness, support, help, loyalty, and faithfulness.

Armorbearing in the attitude of service is not just the performing of humble tasks, but is an effort to serve Christ in the Kingdom of God. Jesus said, "The servant of all is the greatest of all." Among my favorite examples, are the great men in Old Testament scripture, many who were faithful armorbearers before their public ministry. King David, King David's mighty men, Elisha and Joshua exemplified the armorbearing spirit in excellence. Even Elisha's assistant, Gehazi, offers us an example of what we do not want to do as an armorbearer.[6]

One need not think our Father God only called armorbearers or helpers to assist in the ancient battles. Look at New Testament Joseph of Cyprus, nicknamed "Barnabas," or "Son of Encouragement." The most popular view is that Joseph of Cyprus gained these names because he constantly encouraged those to whom he and Paul ministered. Recently, I have considered another thought as to why he was called "Son of Encouragement." Perhaps it was because he persevered by Paul's side through shipwrecks, stoning and much rejection.

Do not overlook Stephen and Phillip among the seven appointed to wait tables for the early church apostles' feeding program. The leaders assigned them to help while their apostles gave greater focus to prayer and the ministry of the Word. Throughout the Bible and today, God is still calling helpers and armorbearers to lift up the arms of our Church leadership.

Operating in the spirit of armorbearing is fulfilling a ministry of helpfulness, watchfulness, and intercession on behalf of our leadership. I believe God has issued a fresh call to serve and support our leaders in this way. Only He knows the spiritual effort and sheer hard work it will take to accomplish the vision of His Church. The Apostle Paul encouraged us to excel in the gifts that build up the Church. As we in the ministry of helps excel in the gift of service and supporting our leaders, we will come into the unity of faith like never before. When we each take our place and share the load our men and women in leadership will suffer less weariness and burnout, giving opportunity for a greater refreshing from the Lord.

Pattern Your Service

King David offers the best example to pattern our armorbearing in the beginning. It was the first position in which David operated in King Saul's service. In addition, he offers a good example of the qualifying spirit to gain if God has called you to operate in the spirit of an armorbearer. Some qualities that brought David before King Saul were:

- *Devotion.* God was able to qualify David because of his devotion to Him first. Secondly, he was obedient and faithful in the secret places. Is your devotion in the right order? Is God first, family, work, and then ministry?

- *Victorious.* David developed a victorious spirit by conquering each challenge as it came. He conquered the bear and lion before he faced the giant, Goliath. Remember your victories as you overcome challenges one day at a time.

- *Respect.* David was reverent and respectful of the ordained office of his leadership (king). Be an example; give respect to the God-ordained office you are serving.

- *Courage.* David counted the cost and took his place in service. Let us count the cost of our service and take our place.

God used these qualities to qualify David for his armorbearer's service to the king. We can use the same qualities in making sure we are qualified for the call of God on our lives. Throughout this book, we will examine other examples, some good, and others offering an example of what not to do. Sometimes it is just as expedient to know what not to do, as it is to realize what to do.[7]

Things Worth Remembering

The basic attitude of a modern day armorbearer is one of servanthood. Therefore, it's no surprise the general functions of an armorbearer: *attend to, minister to, care for, help, be of use, assist, benefit, promote, support, make easy for, nourish and encourage* are found in the formal definition of "serve".[8] Whether you are assigned as a personal armorbearer, or one God has designated to operate in the spirit of armorbearing toward your leaders, remember to:

- *Attend to your leaders by supporting them in spirit and body.* If your leader is ministering, resolve to be there in support. The time is over for our excuses of "I was there with you in spirit." Let your support be in spirit and body.

- *Minister to them as your ministry.* See the support of your leaders as ministry. Remember, God does and so should we.

- *Care for them with God's compassion for His servants.* Be moved with God's compassion for your authorities. Your pastors and church leadership are people—and people need care.

- *Help, be of use, and assist them in the practical.* Be practical in your service. A past leader of mine would often instruct our team with, "Don't be so spiritual that you are no earthly good!"

- *Serve to their benefit.* Our society has become a self-centered world. Go against the natural flow; let your service be to the benefit of your leaders.

- *Promote them.* Be one of their biggest cheerleaders. Everyone needs encouragement. We all enjoy someone who is enthusiastically for us. Be that excited someone to your leadership.

- *Give them the gift of support.* God has ordained a chain of support in ministry. He has called leaders and supporters. Be a part of that chain; link up with your leadership in support.

- *Be one that nourishes and encourages them.* To nourish is to refresh another. According to Webster's Dictionary, "refresh" means to make a person feel stronger, replenished, stimulated or revived.[9] Serve your leaders as one sent to make them stronger, replenished, and revived.

Armorbearing Cultivated

Father God sets armorbearers in place. There is a call for His people to know and operate in the spirit of armorbearing and support throughout the Body of Christ. A powerful principle of God says, "Don't despise small beginnings." In serving, as with all things, start where you are. To begin to develop the spirit of armorbearing in your life:

- *Open your heart to a different perspective on serving.* Just because it is different does not mean it is new. I have learned there is nothing new under the sun.[10] Bernice Fitz-Gibbon commented, "Creativity often consists of merely turning up what is already there. Did you know that right and left shoes were thought up only little more than a century ago?" God desires to take us, the Body of Christ, to new levels. However, the only way we can go is together with a stronger support of each other and our leadership.

- *Accept your high call to ministry and the anointing to serve.* God has a designated ministry and anointing for the people who carry out the details. He has called us to support one another and more specifically, our leaders.

- *Choose God's view of servanthood.* He has a value system that is quite different, if not opposite, of the world's value of a servant. He esteems them as the greatest. With our view of serving, often agreeing with the world's view of an insignificant person doing common tasks, there may be surprises when we see who's given the greatest rewards in heaven.

- *Understand the flow of authority.* God has ordained all authority. Everything works better if you learn to flow in and under authority.

- *Be the gift of support.* God has given a support system to His leaders as a gift. Decide to be a part of this gift of support.

Daily Life

The local prophet of Israel declared the destiny of the young boy standing in the wings of life, waiting to be positioned for service. The young man marked his days by faithfully tending and caring for his father's sheep. He developed a victorious spirit and a heart of bravery by conquering each challenge as it came. When the lion and bear came to steal the sheep, he conquered them. These victories qualified him for greater service. God had taken His Spirit away from the land's king because of disobedience. "Surely there must be someone that could bring me relief from this torment," said the king. One of his elders, moved by God, thought of a young man who fit the description of what they were looking for. He proceeded to give the king the young man's qualifications: a man of courage, a warrior, an attractive person, and the Lord is with him. The rest is biblical history. King Saul chose David to work for him in the palace. He later became the king's favored armorbearer. David was faithful to the daily processes of tending and fighting for his father's sheep. By being faithful with the small, he exemplified the true spirit of armorbearing.[11]

QUESTIONS FOR THOUGHT

---

1. Have you begun with the small of what God has called you to do?

2. What daily processes are you being faithful to in your position of service?

3. Have you realized your obedience to today's process is what qualifies you for tomorrow's power in God?

2

FULFILLING YOUR HIGH CALL TO MINISTRY

o o o o o o o o o o o o o o o o o o o o o o o o o o o o o o o

*And God hath set some in the church, first apostles, secondarily prophets, thirdly teachers, after that miracles, then gifts of healings, **helps**, governments, diversities of tongues.*

—1 Corinthians 12:28 KJV

The ministry gifts such as apostles, prophets, evangelist, teachers, and pastors receive much acclaim and recognition, as it should be. The Body of Christ needs every office set in the Church by God. However, there is a ministry not mentioned as much also set in the Body by our Lord. That is the ministry of helps. There is an important service call for the ministers of helps. Tommy Tenney in his book *God's Secret to Greatness* encourages us with, "The apostle Paul included the "ministry of helps" in his list of supernatural ministries in the Church that are ordained and empowered by God." [1]

How would the church manage without the hands that help? When something practical needs to be done, a person anointed to help steps in and sees to it that the job is completed. God is practical and good and so are they that help.[2] The behind-the-scene jobs in the church often go unrecognized. Yet the humble tasks are the ones we benefit from the most.

There are faithful people who maintain the grounds, clean our church, make repairs, do plumbing, assist with the administration, type bulletins, usher, greet, watch babies, make sure the sound and electronics work smoothly, make snacks and food for the church, do dishes or simply help with the details. Praise God for those serving in the ministry of helps.

Pattern Your Service

Elisha, a businessman, was out plowing with twelve yoke of oxen when the call of God came to him. He changed his schedule and his life to accommodate the call of God. Moved and changed, he counted it all as nothing compared to answering God's call. He accepted his call to the ministry of service without knowing the destiny awaiting him. God had already ordained Elisha as the next prophet of the land. There is no record that Elijah told Elisha what God said. After years of faithfully helping his leader, God promoted Elisha as one matured and prepared for the office of prophet.[3] Elisha exemplified several responses to the call of God which we may pattern our service:

- *Immediacy.* He responded immediately.

- *Timeliness.* He organized his affairs: God, family, work, ministry and so on.

- *Attentiveness.* He heard God for himself. He did not go by what others said. Elijah even responded with, "That's between you and God." He followed and served him anyway.

- *Willingness.* He was willing to start with the small. There are few mentions of Elisha after his initial start with Elijah until the very end.

- *Obedient.* He did the details and ordinary tasks of serving his leader Elijah.

I believe there are more Elisha-spirited servants ready to answer the call. God desires more of us who will not be so concerned about our next promotion. He desires servants who are not saying, "O.K. God, I'll do this dish detail, but you better have something good waiting for me." Instead, there must be more of us who are saying, "Here am I, Lord." [3]

Things Worth Remembering

I have discovered that when I have felt like quitting the most, I did not know my high call in this ministry of service. I began to realize that I did not help just because someone asked me. I serve and help because God called and chose me to be a minister of helps.[4] We are the called and chosen followers, now let us be faithful.[5] There are some points to remember that will help us remain faithful to our high call to ministry:

- *Realize God set the ministry of helps in the Church.*[6] Perhaps you have been thinking that you just volunteer and God does not care about the details. Stop! He does. He designed a special place in His Church for the ministry of (details) helps.

- *Know that Jesus called and chose you.* In John 15:16, He said to us, "You did not choose me, but I chose you and appointed you to go and bear fruit—fruit that will last." [7]

- *Discover God looks upon the heart.* Many believe the ones who get the most attention from man are the most important. However, God sees the secret. King David set a principle like this in place in Israel that remains present today, noted in 1 Samuel 30:24, "The share of the man who stayed with the supplies is to be the same as that of him who went down to the battle. All will share alike." [8]

- *Choose to remain faithful.* Faithfulness continues to be a daily choice. Faithful people are faithful by choice. There are many promises that are yes and amen to the faithful of God.

- *Know that God rewards faithfulness.* He does not reward according to the office in which we serve, but according to the faithfulness shown. He is attentive to His faithful servants. He promises to show Himself faithful to the faithful ones.

The Call Cultivated

Through Scripture, we know God placed ministries in the church, not man. [9] A person should not enter the ministry just because someone told them they were suited for it. Let God call you and place you where He wills.[10] I encounter many who say, "I'm called to preach." Yet they do not start with the small God puts before them to qualify them for their calling. When you are answering your call to serve, consider God may want you to spend a season in the ministry of helps before He matures you to your ministry office. Remember Stephen and Phillip, who started in the ministry of helps but later operated as evangelists? They were faithful to help where God assigned them first.[11] Also, I must mention that there were five others assigned to help. There are no other references of them in the Bible. I believe they continued faithfully serving in the ministry of helps.

If you are uncertain of your call to the ministry of helps, ask God to confirm your calling. Apostle Peter admonishes us to be diligent with proving that we really are called and chosen by the Lord.[12] Give all diligence to exercising and developing His virtues *the fruit of the Spirit* (listed below), so that you may be effective and productive in your gifts and calling:

- *Faith.* Exercise your faith at every opportunity. Faith pleases God. Everyone receives a measure of faith to function within whatever gift

God has graced him. He whose gift is practical service, let him give himself to serving according to the proportion of his faith.[13]

- *Virtue.* After exercising your faith, develop virtue, which is spiritual excellence. Daniel, in serving God and exercising his faith, developed an excellent spirit. So much so that he and his fellow Jewish slaves were found ten times better in all respects than the others assigned to the Kings' service.[14]

- *Knowledge.* In developing an excellent spirit, add knowledge. Get to know your Heavenly Father. As we know Him better, we are sure to discover our destiny and what He wants us to do step by step. Paul wrote to the saints in Ephesus, "I keep asking that the God of our Lord Jesus Christ, the glorious Father, may give you the Spirit of wisdom and revelation, so that you may know Him better." [15]

- *Self-control.* In exercising knowledge, develop self-control. We live in a world of steadily decreasing self-control. The number of road rage incidents is evidence to that. More than half of U.S. Adults are over-weight.[16] Many suffer from lack of control in eating habits. Drug abuse and overdose have increased beyond what our ancestors would recognize. In gaining self-control, more and more we learn to put aside our own desires so that we may fulfill God's desires.

- *Patience.* When allowing the Holy Spirit to help you gain more self-control, add patience. I overheard a teacher's advice to his student, "Never pray for patience, because you will get lots of problems with opportunity to learn patience." The student's reply was, "I don't believe that God would send me problems to teach me anything." Look in on what the Apostle Paul writes the Roman Christians, "We can rejoice, too, when we run into problems and trials, for we know that they are good for us—they help us learn to be patient. And patience develops strength of character in us and helps us trust God more each time we use it, until finally our hope and faith are strong and steady." [17] What do you think of the teacher's advice?

- *Godliness.* As you develop patience, put aside your own desires in an increasing measure, so that God may have His way with you in godliness. The Apostle Peter wrote the Jewish Christians and now us, "Obey God, because you are His children; don't slip back into your old ways—doing evil because you knew no better. However, be holy now in everything you do, just as the Lord is holy, who invited you to be His child. He Himself said, 'You must be holy, for I am holy.'" [18]

- *Brotherly affection.* When practicing godliness, develop brotherly affection. Love one another with brotherly affection—as members of one family—giving precedence and showing honor to one another.[19] Love the brotherhood of believers.[20] Pray for God's people with strong purpose. As you pray for the Body of Christ, interceding on their behalf, your concern will become Christ's compassion. Your hands and feet will become Christ's members, reaching out to the saints. Your affection will become Christ's love flowing through you for His Church.[21]

- *Love.* When praying for the church in brotherly affection, finally add love. Let love guide your speech and actions. In my b.c. *before Christ* days, I would often hurt others by just bluntly telling them the truth. If anyone would say anything to me about it, I would respond with, "Well, it was the truth!" After meeting Christ, I continued with this speaking the truth. But each time I did, I would feel so miserable, I was compelled to apologize. Later, after prayer, the Holy Spirit instructed me I could speak the truth, but in love. I discovered that *truth in love* is often silent. Let love guide your actions. The Apostle John wrote to his friends in the faith, "Little children, let us stop just saying we love people; let us really love them, and show it by our actions." [22] Let love guide your life. Grow to love more and more.

The more we add and develop these qualities in our life, the more useful and fruitful we will be to our Master, Lord Jesus. We will become the special vessels prepared and ready for the Master's use. In Paul's second letter to Timothy, he encourages us to be like the expensive dishes in God's house, "If you stay away from sin, you will be like one of these dishes made of purest gold—the very best in the house—so that Christ Himself can use you for His highest purposes."[23]

Daily Life

Agnes Gonzha Bojaxhiu, better known as, Mother Teresa, said, "I accept in the name of the poor," when she was awarded the 1979 Nobel Peace Prize. Before representing the poor, Mother Teresa, a teacher and then a principal, received a "call within a call" during a train ride, in which she felt God directing her to the slums. By the end of her life, she and more than 3,000 sisters, who followed her, were operating a worldwide network of some 350 missions. A fellow nun said about her, "Mother is very ordinary. When people meet her, she surprises them with her ordinariness. But she allows God to work through her, and He has done extraordinary things." God deliberately chooses what we consider ordinary, even foolish, to confound the wise of our world.

QUESTIONS FOR THOUGHT

---

1. What ordinary tasks does God desire to do extraordinary things in your life?

2. Have you overlooked the small, looking for the large?

3.   Are you proving you really are called and chosen by the Lord?

3

ANOINTED TO SERVE

○ ○
Now there are varieties of gifts, but the same Spirit. And there are varieties of ministries, and the same Lord. And there are varieties of administrations, but the same God, who works all things in all persons. But to each one is given the manifestation of the Spirit for the common good.

——*1 Corinthians 12:4-7*

There are different administrations of the gifts. Armorbearing is an administration of the ministry of helps. This ministry of assisting is simply, one called by God to help another in leadership. Could you picture an apostle, prophet, teacher, or pastor operating successfully without an anointing from heaven? Can you picture anyone operating in the gift of healing without an anointing? No, we could not. Therefore, we must not expect our ministers of helps to operate without the anointing. I believe our Heavenly Father has provided an anointing to serve, a divine endowment to serve effectively.

Pattern Your Service

Stephen and Phillip, two of the first deacons, demonstrated an anointing to serve. They started out waiting tables in the Apostles' feeding program. The Apostles qualified the first deacons with certain qualities that should be present in all who serve. At first glance, the Scripture only says that Stephen and Phillip were filled with the Spirit, wisdom, and faith. After examination, I discovered that with these qualities alone, these men were fully equipped.[1] Look with me in the Book of Acts chapter 6 at what the Scripture says about these servants and their anointing. In doing so, we will know what it requires to operate effectively in the anointing to serve:

- *Holy Spirit.* God chose Stephen and Phillip to serve, yet they walked in tremendous power and anointing of the Holy Ghost. To walk effectively in the anointing, we must allow the Holy Spirit to fill us; the same Holy Spirit that Jesus promised to send to help us, counsel us, and guide us in truth.[2] The Holy Spirit that empowers us to obey Christ will empower us to serve our Lord. An anointing from the Holy Spirit will evidence your service.[3]

- *Wisdom.* The apostle James instructed us, if a man were considered wise, it would be evidenced by his good life and by his actions done in humility. As he further explained wisdom, we can know that Stephen and Phillip served with a pure heart. They were peaceful, considerate of others, submitted to authority and merciful. They served wholeheartedly with sincerity and without selfish agendas.[4]

- *Faith.* Saul of Tarsus was still breathing out threats to the early Church at the time these servants of God came along. The largest portion of the New Testament Scripture had not yet been written, however Stephen and Phillip were full of faith. They exemplified their faith by what they did. Stephen was noted for his working of miracles among the people. Phillip's faith exemplified his ability to follow the leading of the Holy Spirit. Jesus promised us that we could do the same marvelous acts of faith and even greater, "...anyone who has faith in Me will do what I have been doing. He will do even greater things than these, because I am going to the Father...You may ask Me for anything in My name, and I will do it."[5]

Just as any other ministry, it takes more than natural ability to effectively fulfill the ministry of serving. It takes an anointing (a supernatural enablement) from the Holy Spirit. We may pattern our service after men full of the Holy Spirit, wisdom, and faith walking in the anointing of the Lord.

Things Worth Remembering

Most people think of the anointing as something mystical that either you have or do not have. On the other hand, many mistakenly think God's power to do only rests upon those who publicly minister—preach, teach, prophesy, etc. I have heard it often said of someone, "He's not anointed to do anything. He has no ministry." Yet, when I see this person operating in their gifts of administration, I see the anointing. When I observe them doing the work of the ministry of helps, I recognize the anointing to serve. God's anointing empowers you to do whatever He calls you to do. If the Holy Spirit has gifted you to serve, begin to recognize the anointing. Know that you have the anointing and equipment to do all that God created you to be and do. The anointing will:

- *Empower you to discern what needs to be done*

- *Empower you to do the practical*

- *Empower you to do the unlikely*

- *Empower you to give the word of encouragement*

- *Empower you to nourish*

- *Empower you to anticipate needs*

- *Empower you to go the extra mile*

Know that wherever God has called you to serve, He has provided a supernatural enablement to accomplish His work.

The Anointing Cultivated

God's gifts and callings are with out repentance, but the anointing may decrease and fade.[6] I compare the anointing with the talents Jesus spoke of in His parable of the talents.[7] The master gave one man a level one measure of anointing. Another received a level two anointing. Yet, another was given a level five anointing, each according to his ability. Two of them used what he gave them and it multiplied. The one that received the level one anointing did not use his anointing and suffered great loss. Kenneth Hagin recommends going to the Lord if the fires of your anointing wane. He remarks, "I went to the Lord about my anointing decreasing. He told me, 'If your anointing decreases, fast and pray until it comes back.' Now whenever the anointing fades, I wait upon the Lord in prayer and fasting and the same anointing comes upon me again."[8] To keep your zeal and anointing burning hot:

- *Keep your first love first.* We do well to remember the warning given to the Laodicean church, "I know your deeds that you are neither cold nor hot. I wish you were either one or the other! So, because you are lukewarm—neither hot nor cold—I am about to spit you out of my mouth." [9]

- *Protect your anointing.* We protect our anointing by living a holy *separated, consecrated* life. Our Father God requires that we be holy as He is holy.[10] In my own life, God has gifted and anointed me to the discerning of spirits. He often enables me to see into the spiritual realm. The Holy Spirit has instructed me to guard my eyes (being careful what I allow them to see) as a part of the protection of the anointing in my life.

- *Become a student of the Bible.* Study to show yourself a workman approved unto God and rightly dividing the truth. Many men of God started out great, but ended up religious fanatics because they became imbalanced somewhere along the way. All Bible and no Holy Spirit will lead you off the path. On the other hand, all trying to be led by the Holy Spirit and no Word will leave you equally imbalanced.

- *Live a fasted lifestyle.* Deny your flesh all it wants, often. The Apostle Paul admonished us in the race of life, "I make my body do what I want it to do so that after I have preached to others, I myself will not be disqualified." [11]

- *Walk in love.* How can we love God and not love our fellowman? Again, we gain instruction from the Apostle Paul simply paraphrased, "The gifts are useless in your life if you don't have love." [12]

- *Live prayerfully.* Jesus went apart often to pray and listen to the Father. We must follow His example to continue to walk in His anointing. Prayer prepares you for anointed service. Additionally, it helps you continue in anointed ministry. Get to know God in prayer and get to know His plans of service for you. [13]

Daily Life

Carman, a Christian recording artist, while visiting his sister as an east coast Italian kid, black Afro, silk shirt with black slacks, was radically saved (born-again) at an Andrae Crouch concert. His beginning in Christ is where songs like *Serve the Lord* and *No Way Not Ashamed* came from. He admits, "I know what it's like to serve. I served in my local church for about six years before going full time in the music ministry. Those were hard years sometimes. However, I would not trade them because it taught me ministry. It taught me how to identify the Spirit of God. It taught me where and when the anointing was present. I learned when and when not to minister. Through serving, I learned how to accomplish great things in the Kingdom of God. Any person who has ever done anything great for the Lord has dedicated years to the Lord. If you can handle the details, the mundane things of ministry, you can accomplish great things for God."

QUESTIONS FOR THOUGHT

---

1. Have you realized you are developing your anointing through the details of service?

2. What has God empowered you to do through His anointing?

3. What has God led you to do to protect the anointing in your life?

4

CHOOSING GOD'S VIEW OF SERVANTHOOD

○ ○

Having gifts (faculties, talents, qualities) *that differ according to the grace given us, let us use them: He, whose gift is practical service, let him give himself to serving.*

——Romans 12:6-7 AMP

I n the service industry, serving is an art that has lost its value in our society. Few have standards that remain high. Many hold the viewpoint that servanthood is a position. Servanthood is an attitude. It is an attitude that God holds high. In the Body of Christ, Jesus is our chief example, He not counting Himself equal with God, took on the very nature of a servant.[1] How much more should we the Body of Christ do the same? Servanthood is an attitude for the entire Church in which each gift and ministry must seek to continue.

Some in the Body of Christ have a distorted view of servanthood. They view it as a position. In their eyes, most servants are not too bright and inferior to others. I remember washing dishes and cleaning up after serving our pastoral team one day, when a couple came by to say hello. They were extremely condescending saying, *"Ahh!* There are the dishwashers, faithfully washing dishes." They repeated the statement several times. It was not what they said; it was how they said it. Even so, my husband, Varn, and I smiled and kept working.

After they left, I had a feeling of degradation come against me. I felt less than my fellow ministers did. I began thinking, "Wasn't there something better in the Church we could be doing?" I finally said to Varn, "Are we just dishwashers? Do you ever feel ashamed washing the dishes every Sunday?" He said adamantly, "No! And you shouldn't either. That is the devil talking to you. We are blessed. What we are doing is Kingdom business. We are serving as if Jesus had just eaten from these dishes."

When I considered his words, I agreed. The Apostle Paul encouraged the Ephesus church with similar language, "Serve wholeheartedly, as if you were serving the Lord, not men."[2] In God's Kingdom, we handle things differently than in the world. Man looks on the outward appearance, but God looks upon the heart. The world often views the servant as wimpy, despised, and inferior. God's views them as great, purposeful, meek (strength under control), humble and faithful.

Pattern Your Service

According to the writer of I Chronicles, those chosen to serve as gate-keepers of the House of God were selected based on their genealogies, family of Levites, and because of their reliability.[3] Their appointed positions of trust continue to give us insight to what God requires in His New Covenant servants. They exemplified simple qualities that are relevant to our service today:

- *Faithfulness.* The Lord is faithful to the faithful. Did your ancestors serve God? If so, carry the torch in your generation. If not, start a record of faithfulness to God in your family. *In earlier times, Phinehas, son of Eleazar, was in charge of the gatekeepers, and the Lord was with him.*[4]

- *Reliability.* We know that we can rely and depend on God. However, can He depend and rely on our service in His modern day House (Church)? *They were chosen from their villages on the basis of their genealogies, and they were appointed by David and the prophet Samuel because of their reliability.*[5]

- *Trustworthiness.* One of the definitions of trust is 'responsibility resulting from confidence placed in one.' God has trusted us with His gifts and calling. We are responsible (like it or not) for what we do with them. Are we trustworthy of the confidence He has placed in us? *The four head gatekeepers, all Levites, were in an office of great trust, for they were responsible for the rooms and treasuries in the house of God.*[6]

- *Responsibility.* If you are parents of teenagers, you often have to judge if your children are responsible enough to handle certain tasks. Our Father God is the same about us as His children. He will check to see how responsible we are with the small things of the Kingdom before He gives us the weighty tasks. Know that how you handle the anointing you have now, will determine the level of anointing you will operate in tomorrow. *Others were responsible for the furniture, the items in the sanctuary, and the supplies such as fine flour, wine, incense and spices.*[7]

- *Focus.* In our busy lives, it can be difficult to stay focused. It is easy to lose sight of what should be the center of our attention. I have at different times, become too busy in the Lord. Each time to regain my focus, I would go to the Lord to determine what He called me to do and what I agreed to do because it sounded good at the time. Graciously, He would point to His best for me. Let God's best for you be your focus. *The cantors, free from other responsibilities were all prominent Levites. They lived in Jerusalem at the house of God and were on duty at all hours.*[8]

Things Worth Remembering

What is your perspective on servanthood? When you think of servanthood, do you envision it as an activity performed by relatively low-skilled people at the bottom of the positional ladder? Servanthood is not a position it is an attitude. People who have humility can easily be recognized, as well as those without this attitude. We have all encountered a rude waiter in a restaurant, or a utility company employee who does not want to be bothered. The cashier on the phone talking to a friend, instead of helping you is a classic. But wait, let's stop by the Church before we complete the illustration of this point. Have you met an unfriendly greeter? Or perhaps the usher who prods and pushes the sheep into place has prodded you. Then there is the Church employee who has forgotten that they took their job as an opportunity to minister. So what are the qualities that make a person with a serving attitude so easily recognizable?

- *They allow God to purify their motives*

- *They put others ahead of their own agenda*

- *They possess the confidence to serve*

- *They initiate service to others*

- *They are not position conscious*

- *They serve with love and compassion for God's people*

All can easily recognize those that are truly servant-hearted. Are you recognized often as a servant-hearted person?

Serving Cultivated

Even now after many years of serving, I sometimes discover I am doing the right things for the wrong reasons. I thank God that He does not kick us out when we serve with less than pure motives. Yikes! He does not kick us out with any other sin, either. But by His Holy Spirit, He gently shows us where we have gone wrong and the steps to correct it. Where is your heart when it comes to serving others? Do you desire to role-play for advancement? Are you seeking your own way? Or are you truly motivated to help others? In order to improve your attitude of serving, here are a few steps to follow:

- *Perform small acts of kindness.* I agree with those in recent television articles, "There should be more random acts of kindness in our modern world." My father, a farmer, would always seek to have a surplus in vegetables to give to those around him in the community. He would seek out the widows, orphans or that struggling family he heard about in a nearby community. I watched him do this all of his life. James, the Lord's brother, described it as being a part of true religion, "Religion that God, our Father, accepts as pure and fault-less is this; to look after orphans and widows in their distress and to keep oneself from being polluted by the world." [9]

- *Learn to notice others.* An elderly professor in a nursing school sought to teach his students servanthood in the nursing profession. He gave a quiz exam of regular questions, but the last question was, "What is the housekeeper's first name?" Before the class ended, a young woman asked if the last question would count toward their quiz grade. "Absolutely," said the professor. "In your careers, you will meet many people. All are significant. They deserve your attention and care, even if all you do is smile and say hello." Is there someone serving you or with you that you should know more about?

- *Fix your eyes on Jesus.* To develop servanthood in our life, we must take our eyes off ourselves and other people. In the beginning, I found myself being too self-conscious or worrying about what others thought. I have learned to serve by the Spirit. I serve freely, fixing my eyes on the Author and Finisher of my faith, Jesus. [10]

- *Resist serving in bondage.* There is a Scripture that says God is no respecter of persons, therefore, He does not like it when we serve to perform for others. Usually, serving in bondage to perform has to be Holy Spirit revealed. God calls us men-pleasers when we serve our best only to impress others. Scripture has instructed us with, "Whatever you may do, do all for the honor and glory (credit) of God.[11]

- *Serve desiring to give.* I must be transparent and admit that I have served desiring only to receive. As humans, maybe we all have. When we don't receive what we want in return, then we can spiral into negative thinking like, "No one appreciates what I do, no one even said thank you." When I discover this train of thought, I change it to one of thankfulness. I remember it was freely given to me and I freely give. I then can serve, desiring to give, expecting nothing in return.

- *Resist serving on guard.* In life, people can be inconsistent in their behavior and relationships. For a long time, I am sure I wore a sign spiritually that said, "Guard on Duty," as a protection from further hurts. God showed me it was a sin to attempt to be my own protector. I repented. Now, I know Jesus is my Protector and I serve secure because He is consistent yesterday, today and forever.

To Excel in Your Gift of Serving:

Step out of your comfort zone. Strive to serve in those capacities that challenge you, stretch you, and make you grow. Serve even if it makes you uncomfortable for a season. Surprise a few people close to you by doing something for them they would not ordinarily expect from you. Find someone who needs your serving attitude and minister to them. In the ministry and attitude of serving, Jesus set the standard—serving the Father, serving others, and walking in humility. To excel in your gift of serving:

- *Follow Jesus' example*

- *Know God's view of servanthood*

- *Walk in humility*

- *Serve as a slave unto Christ*

Remembering why we do what we do will keep us motivated to remain faithful and serving for the right reason. Re-examine why you do what you do. Discover afresh, Jesus is the best reason for serving. Then go ahead serve your best because you love Jesus.

Daily Life

A young couple fell over backwards on the church auditorium platform, slain in the Holy Ghost, as thousands of people were looking on. Dr. Lester Sumrall had called *Rod and Joni Parsley* forward to receive his mantle of faith. Passing the baton, he publicly imparted to them all that God developed in him over the years. Rod Parsley acknowledged Dr. Sumrall as his mentor, often repeating his advice to him as a young minister to others, "Know your seasons as the chosen of God. There are seasons of receiving, serving and giving." A pastor mentored by Mr. Parsley said, "The only thing I can add to that is: In the season of receiving, you soak up the Word of God like your life depends upon it because it does. In your serving season, you serve like it's your last time you get to because you don't know if it is. Finally, in your giving season, you give in ministry, all you have like the voice of God commanded you to because He has. If you recognize your seasons with God, you will be able to cooperate with His plan and purpose for your life."

QUESTIONS FOR THOUGHT

1. Is your servanthood an attitude?

2. What season are you in as the chosen of God?

3. Are you preparing your service to God as a torch to pass to the next generation?

5

UNDERSTANDING THE FLOW OF AUTHORITY

o o o o o o o o o o o o o o o o o o o o o o o o o o o o o o o

Everyone must submit himself to the governing authorities, for there is no authority except that which God has established. The authorities that exist have been established by God.

——Romans 13:1

Scripture establishes that God has given all authority. There is also a God-given measure of rule, an area, or sphere of rulership. We can act this principle out in our homes, neighborhoods, counties, cities, states, and the nations. There is an authority figure or figures set over each area. Even Satan has implemented this powerful principle in his kingdom of authorities and rulers in the dark world.[1]

All day long, if we are wise, we flow in and under authority. It is essential for an effective helper of the Lord to respect His ordained authority structure. Success will either follow us or elude us according to our submission and even flow in God's order. I have many times spoken with young incarcerated women who have had a problem with authority figures all their lives. I have watched these women sadly realize, so many problems could have been eliminated, if they had gotten the revelation of the flow of authority in their lives, first with their parents and teachers, then with city authorities such as police officers and judges.

We teach our children that the first opportunity for children to obey God is to obey their parents. For all those that have as a child thought, "If I could just be grown-up, I wouldn't have to do what I'm told ever again." Wrong! Even as adults, we continue to flow under and in authority. At home, as a wife, I am under authority. As a mother, I am in authority. As a business owner to my employees, I am in authority. At church, as a church member, I am under the authority of my church leaders. The writer of Romans says, "The authorities that exist have been established by God. Consequently, he who rebels against the authority is rebelling against what God has instituted, and those who do so will bring judgment on themselves." [2]

Pattern Your Service

The centurion, whose servant was sick, applied this authority flow to his faith in Jesus. According to the gospel of Matthew, when the centurion heard that Jesus was in town, he went to Him asking for help. "Lord," he said, "My servant lies at home paralyzed and in terrible suffering." Jesus was ready to go and heal the servant, but the centurion stopped him saying, "...just say the word, and my servant will be healed. For I myself am a man under authority, with soldiers under me. I tell this one, 'Go.' And he goes; and that one, 'Come' and he comes. I say to my servant, 'Do this,' and he does it." Jesus commended the centurion's faith and understanding of authority. Matthew records that the centurion's servant was healed at the same hour he asked. The centurion offers us a simple pattern of understanding the flow of authority instituted by God.[3]

Things Worth Remembering

We must be willing to apply this principle of authority to the authority God has set in our lives. It may be parental authority, church authority, school authority, work or governmental authority. No one is exempt from being under authority and accountable to an authority in his or her life. In addition, no one remains accountable to authority by accident. It requires a decision. Webster's dictionary tells us *account-able* means: being responsible, liable, or explainable.

All levels of our life and relationships need accountability. Even so, not many people truly enjoy being accountable. We don't always enjoy questions like: Where were you last night? Where were you on Sunday morning? Why did you handle it like that? Is there any money left in the account? Our flesh (human nature) enjoys being question-free about what it is doing or not doing.

Those in authority hold us accountable in our lives. Parents hold their children accountable, spouses hold each other accountable, employers hold their employees' accountable, governing agencies hold employers accountable, and so on. We, the family of God, hold each other accountable in Christ. Father God holds us all accountable.

The Flow of Authority Cultivated

By submitting to authority in our life, we become accountable. In fact, where we see *submit,* it can be interchanged with *be accountable.* For example, let's view how it would work in the Church with some of the verses including *submit.*[4]

- Submit (be accountable) to one another out of reverence for Christ.[5]

- Obey your leaders and submit (be accountable) to their authority.[6]

- Young people, be submissive (accountable) to those who are older.[7]

Accountability creates boundaries and safeguards to our path, much like the guardrails and side supports of our highways. Often in reviewing the fall of our Christian leaders in recent years, you can usually follow their path to demise and note a lack of accountability in their lives. As I stated earlier, accountability is a choice, especially as you mature in leadership. The people you are around the most may report to you in authority. Therefore, an effort must be made to remain accountable. We must find someone we look up to spiritually and submit to their authority, allowing them to be a voice of accountability in our lives.

To develop and maintain accountability in your life, regardless of the level of authority in which you serve, embrace these principles:

- *Understand the flow of authority.* The centurion in Jesus' day recognized and understood the flow of authority for him.

- *Stay humble.* Humility will keep the door open for accountability.

- *Seek accountability.* As you mature in leadership, it will be worth the effort.

- *Stay involved in mentorship.* Allow mentorship to flow in your life. Mentoring and being mentored will hold accountability in place in your life.

God wants renewed respect for His authority structure. In years past, a number of large ministries have fallen, bringing negative attention to the Kingdom of God. Through the failures of the few, many of us have become hardened and cynical, pointing the finger (stereotyping). For example, it is commonly said that all television evangelist are "Mr. Wonderfuls" and after your money. All pastors with super large congregations are greedy. Many have lost respect for our men and women of God.

When Jesus asked Ananias to go to a blinded Saul on the road to Damascus, with good reason, Ananias reminded Him of what Saul had been doing against the Saints of God. Jesus responded with, "I will make it clear to him how much he will be afflicted and must endure and suffer for My name's sake." [8]

We could easily point out what our most popular ministers have visibly gained. What about the sacrifices that only God knows about? I believe we must renew respect for the call and anointing of God upon our ministers.

I have purposed to look at our ministers with fresh eyes of compassion. Join me, let's choose together to remember and honor them for the life they have chosen for Christ's sake. Make a new commitment, as I do, to pray for our leaders and those in authority.[8]

Daily Life

His father and mother were beginning to worry. They had looked everywhere and checked with everyone they knew, but still no Jesus. Finally, they made it back to the last place they had seen their son. There he was, sitting among the scribes and Pharisees in the temple, asking and answering difficult questions.

"Why did you do this to us," they asked Him.

"Did you not know I had to be about My Father's business?" He replied.

Then the Scripture declared, after this He went with His parents and was obedient to them, submitting to their authority.[9]

QUESTIONS FOR THOUGHT

---

1. Are you a leader, yet flowing in and under authority?

2. Name three people to whom you are accountable.

3. How similar are you to the centurion?

6

BEING THE GIFT OF SUPPORT

o o o o o o o o o o o o o o o o o o o o o o o o o o o o o o o
*"But bring your brothers, the tribe of Levi, to join you and serve
you while you and your sons minister before the Tent of the Testimony. They are to serve you and take care of the details of the
Tent. I myself have selected your fellow Levites from among the
Israelites as a gift to you, dedicated to the Lord to take care of the
details at the Tent of Meeting."*

——Numbers 18:2, 3, 6 paraphrased.

Are you serving in a support position on your team or ministry?
Determine to let your service be a gift. Know that you are a gift to
the Body of Christ and the Body of Christ is a gift to you. The Apostle
Peter admonished us with, "Each one should use whatever gift he has
received to serve others, as good stewards of the manifold grace of
God...whoever serves, let him do so as by the strength which God
supplies.[1]

In the Old Testament, God gave the Levites' help as a gift to Aaron
and his sons. It was not earned for Aaron was not any more deserving
than we are of God's gifts to us. God, in His mercy, designed a chain of
support still active today. He literally called out the Levites solely as a
support ministry to the priesthood and offered them to Aaron and his
sons as a gift.[2]

Pattern Your Service

God's design and purpose for our Levite brothers reflect a beautiful pattern for his New Testament servants today. God set the Levites apart and their practical ministry offered as a gift.

> *I myself have selected your fellow Levites from among the Israelites as a gift to you, dedicated to the Lord to take care of the details at the Tent of Meeting.*
> —— *Num. 18:6*

They were to help the men of God and take care of all the details of the Tent. Look with me at some simple principles set forth that will undergird and still apply to our modern day support ministries:

- *God appointed the Levites.* He selected the Levite brothers from among the other Israelites to join Aaron and his sons in service. In a similar fashion, the writer of the first book of Corinthians tells us, "God chooses and puts His saints exactly where he wants them in the Body of Christ. [3] I believe it is worth injecting, if we allow him.

- *The Lord dedicated the Levites to Himself.* One of the meanings given for dedication as well as holy is 'set apart'. Interchanging the words we could say, "The Levites were set apart for the Lord." The Apostle Peter reminds us of an Old Testament command that still applies to God's servants today saying, "Be holy as I am holy." [4] Join me as I ask myself, "How set apart am I to the Lord for service in His Church?"

- *God gave the Levites' ministry as a gift.* What a wonderful honor given to the Levite tribe of Israel. When I prepare a gift for my child, I make sure it is the best quality that I can find. The physician Luke phrased it in a similar way referring to God's gifts saying, "If your nature is evil and you know how to give good gifts to your children, how much more will your Father in heaven give a good gift." [5] The helps ministry is a gift to our ministry leaders in the Church. Let us endeavor to walk worthy of this calling.

• *God assigned the Levites to the details of the Tent.* They were given duties concerning the Tent while the priest ministered before the Lord. Perhaps the early Church apostles had this fact in mind when they assigned the first seven to handle the details of ministry while they spent more time before the Lord in prayer and the ministry of the word. Have you been assigned the details of the ministry while your leadership ministers before the Lord? If so, know that you have been given a great honor.

Things Worth Remembering

God presented the support ministries to His people as a gift. Through the writer of Exodus, it was revealed that Aaron was called to support Moses.[6] Now it's clear that the Levites were called to support Aaron. In the New Testament, we see an example in the first deacons of the church, men called to serve the people; especially widows and orphans while, the Apostles prayed and ministered the Word. God has designed a chain of support. Look at God's chain of support in the Old Testament versus our local Church body:

God called Moses to lead the Israelites	God called Senior Pastors to lead Church Body
God called Aaron to be Moses' helper and associate priest	God called pastoral staff to assist Senior Pastors
God called Levites to minister to priesthood	God called helps ministry to help ministry leaders
God called Israelites to support priest & Levites	God called congregation to support leadership team

We need each other in God's chain of support. We must begin to take our place and serve as a strong link in God's chain. As an example look again to the book of Exodus, the Israelites were in a battle with the Amalekites.[7] Moses went to the top of a mountain and held the staff out over the battle. As long as his arms were up, the Israelites prevailed. However, when his hands were down, the Amalekites were winning. Aaron and Hur put a large rock under Moses for him to sit on. Then one stood on each side to hold his arms up in the air.

God could have supernaturally strengthened Moses' arms to the point where he did not need Aaron and Hur to hold them up. I believe God wanted to spotlight our need for each other, especially in times of battle. Pastor Gordon Banks phrased it like this, "Working alone in Jesus, you may eventually win. But working together in Jesus, you win quickly." Often without support, our personal battles are longer than necessary. In addition, if we do not allow others to share in our battle, we cheat them of their share in the joy of victory. Jesus spoke of this when He said, "Those that share in My sufferings, I will share My glory with them." [8]

Gift of Support Cultivated

Have you ever thought of yourself as a gift to the body of Christ, specifically God's leaders? Realize your support means that much in God's plans. A short illustration of our sometimes-wrong thinking is: The eyes of the body said sarcastically to the ears, "We can do all the seeing around here. We do not really need you. Besides, you are just an ear. You sit all the way on the side of the head. Not in front like all eyes do." The ears responded, "I guess I'm not needed. Hair hides me most of the time. I suppose God just put me here on the side and forgot about me…" [9] Does that scenario sound like someone who has lost the value of his or her unique purpose?

In referring to the illustration above, the body would be handicapped without the function of the ears. Furthermore, it is not as if the eyes can effectively serve the purpose for which the ears are created. In the same way, we must realize no one can effectively fulfill our unique purpose given by God. The Apostle Paul confirmed this to the Corinthian church saying, "Now here is what I am trying to say: All of you together are the one body of Christ and each one of you is a separate and necessary part of it." If you have not already, begin to develop your support as a gift. To strengthen right perspective, you must include the points below in your thinking:

- *Recognize its God's way of doing things.* He has ordained the Body of Christ to need each other.

- *Determine to be a link in His chain of support.* We can choose to be a strong link or a weak link in His chain.

- *Treat your support as a gift.* When we offer our service as a gift, we don't expect return favors.

- *Connect with others who serve.* Remember a link connects with others to become a strong chain. We link arms with those who serve and strengthen God's system of support for our leaders. Do not break the chain.

Daily Life

Moses was a great leader who spoke the oracles of God. He served in the office of prophet and judge. God commended him as His friend and the most humble man on earth. He was assigned to one of the greatest tasks in human history, leading approximately one million Jews out of slavery. Yet, he was frail in some aspects. He was a human like us. He needed help. God assigned Aaron to help him and the chain of support began. Somehow, he and Aaron could only go so far alone. God designated Joshua to pull in close to help Moses and strengthen the chain. He appointed the seventy elders, giving them of the spirit that was on Moses. However, the chain was not complete. During battle with the

Amalekites, Hur was called in concert with Aaron to help. They held up Moses' arms together. Then God assigned the priesthood of Levites to support these two and share duties in the House of God. Finally, God called the whole congregation of Israelites to help this team of leadership and to complete the chain of support.[11]

QUESTIONS FOR THOUGHT

---

1. Are you a link in God's chain of support?

2. How can you make your connection with others stronger in His system of support?

3. Is your service a gift to the Body of Christ; if not what can you do to make it so?

7

DEVELOPING THE SPIRIT OF ARMORBEARING

○ ○

And I will come down and talk with thee there: and I will take of the spirit which is upon thee, and will put it upon them: and thy shall bear the burden of the people with thee, that thou bear it not thy alone.

——Numbers 11:17

A local television station in Texas has adopted its slogan as 'in the spirit of Texas'. Because of the strong sense of state pride in Texas, it has become very popular. This sense of comradelier goes all the way before the Alamo to the Texican settlers. During a commercial produced by this station, they show a succession of multi-cultural spokespersons, each describing what the pervading quality or spirit of Texas is to them. For one, it was the sense of community, or the "bigness" of Texas. To another, it was their good Texan neighbors, excellent education, or the entrepreneurship of Texans.

In a simile, I have gathered a succession of biblical characters, each displaying a pervading quality of armorbearing. In chapters one through six, we have examined David's qualifying attitude, Elisha's answer to God's call and his devotion and Stephen and Phillip's humility and power with God. We introduced the Israelite gatekeepers' trusted responsibilities, the centurion's understanding of authority and the Levite's gift of support. We may pattern our service from this simile.

Pattern Your Service

There is a young man that especially exemplified the spirit of armorbearing in his actions. His name was Baruch, assistant to Prophet Jeremiah. Prophet Jeremiah and Baruch lived during a time that God was judging His people for their continued disobedience. The times were evil and many times Jeremiah was thrown in jail for the message from God he was compelled to give. From jail, he continued to dictate God's Words to his assistant Baruch. Baruch, following Jeremiah's instructions would go to the temple and read the Word of God to the people. Even though Baruch, a human like us, grew weary with all the accusations and persecutions that came along with serving one of God's leaders, he remained faithful. God sent him a word of encouragement to remain thankful for his life. For in the midst of all the trouble He was sending upon his chosen nation He promised to protect him wherever he went as a reward. Baruch offers us a model of courage, obedience, and faithfulness in serving God's leader.[1]

Things Worth Remembering

In any administration of the helps ministry, one may operate in the spirit of armorbearing. In the first chapter, armorbearer was traced to the Hebrew word *nasa,* meaning to support or simply help. With this in mind, anyone may operate in the spirit of helping someone in leadership. No title is needed to lift up the arms of God's leaders. Perhaps you are one of those God has called from the pew to simply start where you are, helping your leadership. As one operating in the spirit of armorbearing, remember to develop the qualities found in servanthood:

- *Be attentive.* Watch for and observe your leaders' needs. Most may be in the mindset that all is taken care of in the Church. However, if you look with a discerning eye, God will lead you where to lend a hand.

- *Minister to your leadership.* Treat your service as ministry. God will show you where you are needed most. Remember He puts each person just where He wants him or her to be.[2]

- *Care for God's servants.* Flow in His compassion for your leaders. Take on the advice of the apostle Peter, "And now this word to all of you: You should be like one big happy family, full of compassion for each other, loving one another with tender hearts and humble minds." [3]

- *Assist your leaders in the practical.* The helps ministry is a practical ministry. God inspires our authorities with a great plan or vision but they need your help with the details.

- *Serve to their benefit.* God calls us men pleasers if we serve only to impress others. Examine your service. Is it to your leaders' benefit or to your benefit only?

- *Empower your leaders.* In a self-centered society, it can be difficult to find people who are willing to lay aside their needs to attend to another. The writer of John instructs with, "Greater love has no one than this that he lay down his life for his friend." [4] You can do it, lay self aside, and promote another. As you do so, God will certainly empower you and promote you in due season.

- *Be the gift of support to them.* Acknowledge God has set you in place to support your leaders. Know that you come highly recommended by the Father. You are the gift of support.

- *Nourish and encourage your leadership team.* Do not always get in the receiving line. Mature and know that God is your ultimate source. Be prepared for God to use you to offer nourishment and encouragement to your leaders.

The Spirit of Armorbearing Cultivated

In refining silver or gold, the metal is put through intense heat, more than several times to remove dross and impurities. Each time, the gold or silver comes out improved, more clear, and precise. There are ways to refine the spirit of armorbearing. To improve the spirit of armor bearing in your life:

- *Initiate service.* Don't wait to be asked, volunteer. Jesus told a story likening the Kingdom of God to a landowner who went out early in the morning to hire men to work in his vineyard. He went out and hired men four different times during the day to work. The final time and the final hour he went out asking the men, "Why have you been standing here all day long doing nothing?" 'Because no one has hired us,' they answered.[5] One of the many times I've read this story, I heard Jesus saying to me, "It is the final hour, why are you sitting in My Church doing nothing?" "Because no one has asked me," I responded. Have you been waiting to be asked? Don't. Find your place and volunteer.

- *Maintain a sense of urgency.* A retail district manager in training the managers in his district would drill them constantly saying, "Get the job done and have a sense of urgency!" Finally, one day a young manager raised his hand asking, "What is a sense of urgency?" An older manager replied, "Get everything done like your house is on fire!" Jesus, with a better explanation encouraging His disciples said, "All of us must quickly carry out the tasks assigned us by the One who sent Me, for there is little time left before the night falls and all work comes to an end."[6]

- *Continue to develop the heart of a servant.* Our chief example, Jesus, developed the heart of a servant. During one of His last days on earth, He wrapped a towel around Himself to serve and washed His disciples' feet saying, "I have set you an example that you should do as I have done for you." [7]

- *Be humble.* God resists the proud, but He comes to fellowship with the humble in heart. I have always heard a portion of Scripture quoted by some older members in my family, "Pride comes before a fall…" And yes, it does, but the other part that I can not remember hearing is, "humility comes before honor." [8] Many miss the mark because they strive to be great. I have discovered that as I humble myself, God handles the great part.

- *Be faithful.* Sign up for long-term service, as long as God says stay. For example, the Bible estimates Elisha served Elijah twenty years before Elijah was caught up into the heavens. Joshua served Moses over 40 years before Moses went up into the mountains never to come down again. I am not implying you must serve your leaders until they die, just until God says it's time to move on.

- *Stay submitted to authority.* Lack of continued submission to authority may be the biggest cause of turnover among the ranks of God's army. Many times people simply get tired of following. A couple who were friends of mine grew weary waiting on God. Impatiently, they thought their leaders would not acknowledge them. They left the Church and later came back saying, "We quickly realized we had made a mistake by rebelling against authority." [9]

- *Know there will be persecution.* Our enemy, the devil, knows the importance of people fulfilling their call to help and support God's leaders. Therefore, he stirs up trouble against God's servants. In Paul's charge to Timothy, he said, "Everyone who wants to live a godly life in Christ Jesus will be persecuted." [10] In the same manner, our Chief Servant encouraged us with, "If the world hates you, keep in mind that it hated Me first...No servant is greater than his master. If they persecuted Me, they will persecute you." [11]

- *Guard against jealousy, familiarity, and offense.* A saying that has become a proverb among the Saints of God says, "If the devil can't get you to go back to sin in the streets of the world, he will subtly try to entrap you with sins of the heart." Sins like jealousy, pride, offense or familiarity (insubordination) will soon invite our own downfall.[12]

- *Say no to criticism of your leaders.* One of the most accurate darts of the enemy to harm our leaders is the arrow of criticism, many times fashioned by our (the Church) own lips. In the desert, the whole community criticized Moses and Aaron...Moses also said, "Who are we? You are not criticizing us, but the Lord." Then Moses told Aaron, "Say to the entire Israelite community, 'Come before the Lord, for he has heard your complaining.'" [13]

- *Follow the basics of faith.* We know we must love and walk in forgiveness. A teacher and businessperson in our Church says, whenever she faces trouble, she goes back to the ABC's of faith (the things she learned in the beginning). The writer of Hebrews put it like this, "Let us stop going over the same old ground again and again, always teaching those first lessons about Christ. Let us go instead to other things and become mature in our understanding, as strong Christians ought to be." [14]

Daily Life

How would you like your reputation in the ministry of serving to follow you the rest of your life? That is what happened to *Elisha*. He had developed faithfulness, loyalty, integrity, and strength of character through the ministry of serving Elijah. After Elijah had gone to heaven, three kings in a desperate situation needed to hear the word of the Lord in a hurry. A servant of the king of Israel recommended a man for the job, "Elisha is available. Use him, you know the one who served Elijah." King of Judah, Jehosphaphat said, "Yes, he's the one we want! He has the word of the Lord." Elisha did come and prophesy a word of victory to the three kings. But his reputation as a servant of the man of God, Elijah, identified him and qualified him for this greater service.[15]

QUESTIONS FOR THOUGHT

---

1. Are you called by God to operate in the spirit of armorbearing to your leadership?

2. Would your reputation in the ministry of serving identify you for greater service in God?

3. Do you have a sense of urgency in your service to God?

8

TEN POWER PRINCIPLES OF SERVING

o o o o o o o o o o o o o o o o o o o o o o o o o o o o o o o o o
I have set you an example that you should do as I have done for you.

—*John 13:15*

I n life, we eventually imitate someone we admire. We will aspire to be more like someone. In my high school days, I was a finalist in a contest. As a finalist, the judges asked an impromptu question: Name two people who are alive which you would like to be more like and why. I answered, "I would like to be more like my father because he is the epitome of what I think a good person should be. He is kind, giving, and a good listener. Secondly, but not least, I would like to be more like my Lord Jesus Christ. He died for our sins and as a Christian; I desire His qualities of love for people, compassion for those in need and His giving nature." The judges quickly disqualified my answer because they did not consider Jesus a live person. I knew perhaps my response was not the best phrased, but it did not enter my mind that anyone would consider Jesus as *not alive*. To this day, I still think He is the best person by whom I model my life, behavior, and ministry.

When I began to pray and seek the Lord about being a better servant of Christ through operating in the spirit of armorbearing, He gave me some powerful principles that have changed my outlook on serving in any capacity. These values are dynamite when applied to service in God's house.

1. *Serve as imitators of Christ*

    God seemed to put dissatisfaction in me with the norm...saying, "Son, don't be like other men be like Jesus." *Dr. Oral Roberts.*

    I have set you an example that you should do as I have done for you. *John 13:15*

2. *Serve in step with the Holy Spirit*

    Jesus said to me, "Faith obeys my Word, whether it is the written Word of God or my Spirit, who has spoken to man." *Kenneth Hagin, Sr.*

    Since we live by the Spirit, let us keep in step with the Spirit. *Galatians 5:25, 26*

3. *Serve wholeheartedly*

    God calls us men pleasers when we serve only to impress others. *Earma Brown*

    Serve wholeheartedly, as if you were serving the Lord, not men. *Ephesians 6:7*

4. *Serve in the beginning*

    You don't have to be great to start, but you have to start to be great. *Pastor Keith Davis,*

    Do not despise this small beginning, for the eyes of the Lord rejoice to see the work begin. *Zec. 4:10a*

5. *Serve as a gift of support*

Give the Church your gift of support. *Earma Brown*

When Moses' hands grew tired, they took a stone and put it under him and he sat on it. Aaron and Hur held his hands up—one on one side, one on the other—so that his hands remained steady till sunset. *Exodus 17:12*

6. *Serve willingly*

The world is full of willing people; some willing to work, the rest willing to let them. *Unknown*

For the leaders who took the lead in Israel, for the people who offered themselves willingly, bless the Lord. *Judges 5:2 AMP*

7. *Serve with your eyes on Jesus*

Obstacles are those frightful things you see when you take your eyes off your goal. *Henry Ford*

"Come," He said. Then Peter got down out of the boat, walked on the water and came toward Jesus. But when he saw the wind, he was afraid and, beginning to sink, cried out, "Lord, save me!" *Matthew 14:29,30*

8. *Serve to increase military strength*

When you fight alone in Jesus, you win, eventually. When you fight together in Jesus, you win quickly. *Pastor Gordon Banks*

One shall put a thousand to flight, and two will chase ten thousand. *Deuteronomy 32:30*

9. *Serve to lighten the load of others*

The greatest achievements are those that lighten the load of others. *Unknown*

Carry each other's burdens and in this way, you will fulfill the law of Christ. *Galatians 6:2*

10. *Serve by doing*

Well done is better than well said. *Benjamin Franklin*

His master replied, 'Well done, good and faithful servant! You have been faithful with a few things; I will put you in charge of many. *Matthew 25:23a*

PART II
SERVING GOD'S LEADER

Excellent chapter 9

FROM THE HEART OF AN ARMORBEARER

o o o o o o o o o o o o o o o o o o o o o o o o o o o o o o

"Do all that you have in mind," his armorbearer said, "Go ahead; I am with you heart and soul."

———*1 Samuel 14:7*

Recently, I listened to a friend complain about a Church project using a well-used phrase, "There are too many chiefs and not enough Indians around here. It seems everyone wants to be in charge." My mind drifted as I thought, "How many times have I heard this complaint about various teams over the years. I thought about the need of understanding God's authority structure. It is not a new struggle nor is it isolated to the New Testament Church, as I considered Moses and Aaron's conflict with Israelite grumblers. They had complained against the leadership of Moses and especially Aaron saying, "We are all chosen and holy, who set you above all the Israelites?" Under Old Testament law, judgment and destruction came to many of those who complained. God, in His mercy, approved Aaron's leadership with a budded, blossoming staff with ripe almonds hanging from it among the staffs that stayed the same. He then graciously reiterated the duties of the leaders and the supporters.[1] It is a fact, not everyone is called to be a leader at the same time. Someone must lead and others must follow.

From Scripture, we discovered God appoints leaders and those to support them.

Have you been appointed to support someone in your leadership? Is your heart set toward helping this person accomplish their God-given tasks? If the answer is yes, then you are not alone. All over the Body of Christ, God continues to make specific appointments of helpers to assist His authorities. As an administration of the Helps ministry, He has uniquely formed the armorbearer's place in His support system. It is a part of His design for a team to strengthen His leaders.

When God called my husband and me to serve as armorbearers to our senior pastors, we started looking for good examples. We looked for people who have served or currently serve in the ministry of assisting. We asked the Holy Spirit, our Teacher, to give us examples. We wanted to know the qualities needed to be an effective armorbearer. He showed us examples in name and function. A special one comes to mind, which was not mentioned by name in the Bible, but by his function as Prince Jonathan's armorbearer. He was not involved in the ministry of assisting anyone and everyone. He was assigned to Jonathan. He was focused and attentive to his leader.

When Jonathan is found on top of the hill spying out the enemy's camp, we don't have to look very far to find his helper. He was there with him. Scripture says Jonathan turned to his armorbearer and said, "Let's go up..." His assistant's response was, "Do all that is in your mind. For I am with you heart and soul." [2] Those words are music to any leader's ears, whether he is a weary church leader or a pastor needing an arm of support. I believe the Body of Christ needs those who will support the man or woman of God in a more tangible way. God is looking for people who will be with their assigned leader heart and soul.

Pattern Your Service

Moses had the tremendous task of leading approximately one million Jewish slaves out of Egypt, a lot for any man. Even so, it became clear that God had his back as His design for a support team slowly unfolded. He had called Aaron and Miriam to help him. Then he appointed the seventy elders who partook of his authority and helped him. Aaron's sons were called forward to help with the priestly duties; later the whole Levite tribe was assigned to help in the priesthood. During the battle with the Amalakites, Aaron and Hur stepped forward in unison to hold up Moses' arms in the battle, as *Joshua led the troops to victory.* This was the first mention of Joshua, the man who served Moses in the ministry of assisting. In this instance, he served Moses by being a helper in the battle against God's enemies. The next event, a Holy God summoned Moses to come up the mountain, Joshua was identified as Moses' aide who went with him. He did not come down until Moses did, forty days and nights later. He was also noted for his zeal at the Tent of Meeting. When Moses would go talk with God and return to the camp, Joshua would stay behind in the Tent. He was faithful in this ministry of helping the Lord by assisting Moses for over forty years. Moses' armorbearer Joshua inspires us with an example of a zealous assistant, giving enough intensity and focus to help his leader accomplish the impossible for God. [3]

Things Worth Remembering

As the Holy Spirit began to teach us about armorbearing, He gave us biblical as well as modern-day illustrations. We began to see qualities to model in the most surprising places. My husband and I have an adopted member of our family that exemplifies some of the qualities needed for armorbearing. Our dog is loyal, attentive, and his watchful nature has endeared him to us over the years. Six weeks after he was born, we received his ancestral papers and discovered he came from a long line of loyal Rottweillers. We added Domino's name to his family tree with names like Majestic Rocky Johnston, Grizzly Moon Star, Welkerhaus' Thunder, Midnight, Star, and Boo-Boo Bearess.

Later, we took Domino to an obedience class. May I brag a little? At that time, he was the most obedient member of the class. He sat quietly at our side with this puzzled look, observing the other dogs' behavior. There was another Rottweiller, two dogs down that wanted to bite everything in sight. The owners enrolled in the class as a final effort to bring him in control. Next to us was a huge Dalmatian that acted as if he brought his owner to class; he would not listen to anything she said. In addition, present in the class were two dogs that barked non-stop.

One of the first things our instructor told us (besides how to stop a constantly barking dog) was to <u>bond with our dogs</u>. We could do that by leashing the dog to our side for a day or two. Whatever we did, our dog would be at our side. His instruction was, "<u>If someone broke in on your family</u> you do not want your dog off chewing a shoe, not <u>attentive that you were being attacked.</u>" In our case, somehow we had already bonded with Domino. Whatever we did, he was right there at our side. When we put him outside to play, he would sit at the window and watch what we were doing, obviously desiring to be back inside near us. He is the most watchful and attentive dog we have ever had. Domino offers us a pattern of the simple qualities necessary to possess as an effective armorbearer such as loyalty, watchfulness, and attentiveness.

<u>Another element of effective armorbearing can be the acknowledgement of God's choice.</u> I have realized our choices have everything to do with the Lord's choice. Although the Lord knows His own and He has said, "I chose you, you did not choose yourself," we must accept the call.[4] The moment I acknowledged myself as a God-chosen armorbearer, my self-doubts left and the anointing flowed. There are some key things to remember while growing in the ministry of armorbearing:

- *Recognize God still appoints people to help today.* Then the Lord said to Moses, "See, I have chosen Bezalel son of Uri, the son of

Handwritten margin notes: WE MUSt BONd. PLAY"J, so4. EAtiJ, DRiJJ, WAtcJJ T.V. ✓ A Defeade

Handwritten bottom note: I AM APPoiNted

Hur...And I have appointed Oholiab, son of Ahisamach, of the tribe of Dan to help him." [5]

- *Allow God to make your appointment.* In observing ministry leaders and helpers alike, your assignment may not necessarily be whom you would choose. John C. Maxwell simplifies this principle saying, "Leaders attract not whom they want, but who they are." [6] Even so, God chooses and appoints, for He knows the needs of the ministry and the personalities. He fitly joins leader and helper together, if we allow Him.

  very specific
- *Know your calling will be specific.* God places armorbearers with a designated person in leadership. Your appointment will be specific. Joshua was assigned to Moses, Elisha to Elijah, David to Saul, Timothy to Paul, etc.

  he is worthy.
- *Your leader will be worthy.* He or she will be a faithful servant with proven leadership. More than likely they will be serving in one of the fivefold offices of ministry. God will appoint you to serve one who is faithful.

  its confirmed
- *God will give confirmations.* Let your appointment be established through two or three witnesses.[7] You and your leader will know. Don't be in a hurry. If God has truly called you to a certain person, He will give evidence of your appointment.

  I am not prideful but I am very guarded.
✱
- *Resist pride.* It will oppose your service in the ministry of helps and God will oppose you when you are prideful. Strive to wear humility as a garment.[8]

  what a confirmation.
- *Don't be surprised by persecution.* No servant is greater than his master is. Our Lord was persecuted and His godly servants will be persecuted. Rejoice that you are counted among the godly and prepare for persecution.[9]

I don't need to defend myself.

- *Know God is your defender.* Let's purpose to choose Him as our defense as we serve others.[10] You have laid your armor down to hold another's. In the same way, Christ has said, "There is no greater love, than one to lay down his life for his friends." [11]

God still appoints armorbearers to serve in the ministry of helps today. Your leader needs you. According to Bishop T.D. Jakes in his *Keepers of the Flame* tape series, "Many of our leaders' arms have fallen down, not because they weren't anointed, but because there was no one in place to hold their hands up in the heat of the battle."[12]

Ministry of Assistance Cultivated

With any ministry, gift, or talent God has entrusted us to use, we must develop it to reach its fullest potential. To develop the ministry of helping as an armorbearer, do this:

- *Build relationship.* Get to know whom you are serving. Relationship will guard you. For example, one key thing relationship will guard you against are the baits of Satan (offenses). When he comes to distort the truth about your authority, you can say, "I know this person there must be a reason for this." Your leader may do the same for you through relationship.

- *Personalize your service.* What one leader desires will be different from another. Each pastor or leader has a different set of gifts and needs of service than another. Learn what your leader's are and personalize your service. Allow the Holy Spirit to guide you. Be attentive to his promptings. He will teach you what works best for your authority.

- *Be pure in your service.* Make sure your service is to your leader's benefit. For example, a pastor friend of mine expressed her disappointment at the immaturity of her assistant. She explained, "My

[handwritten top margin: Great Paragraph. WHEN we are going to a church for Him to preach there are so many things on my mind But This is not The time for me to talk about it. He always]

armorbearer insisted she come to my speaking engagement for sup- *[comes to talk to me later]* port. I said great, and then she asked if I would pick her up, which was fine but on the way, I interpreted two dreams, counseled her, *[I always seem to have some time to visit my frustration]* and prayed with her before arriving at the meeting. I was drained before I made it to the platform." I agreed with my friend's frustration regarding the assistant's lack of consideration for her need. Remember, there is a time and place for everything. Allow your concerns and needs to take a backseat to discerning your leader's need. God is faithful; as you plant seeds of excellent service in your leader's life, He will remember to take care of you.

- *Wear godly garments.* Be careful of the attitude you wear when serving your leader. One of my team leaders says often, "I am careful of my attitude and mindset when I serve my leaders because whether I intend to or not I often transfer it to them. I don't want them to have to guard against receiving a bad attitude from me." If we strive to wear a garment of humility, kindness, and congeniality, our leaders may safely trust themselves to us. *[I have to change my attitude when I get around Him regardless of How I feel.]*

- *Develop loyalty in your ministry.* Determine to be where your assigned leader is. Have you considered where Joshua was when Moses went up the mountain to receive the law of God? We can only assume he was somewhere close by because he was right there with him when he came off the mountain forty days later. Remember, how can your ministry to him or her be developed if you are not in place?

[handwritten: This is The reason why I Don't close my eyes when He is praying.]

- *Develop a watchful spirit.* Jesus said to his assistants on the first night of his trial, "Watch and pray…" Yet, they were unable to stay awake to watch. He then gave us the key to a watchful spirit in His last words to them saying, "The spirit is willing but the flesh is weak." [13] If it is your hour of trial or your leader's hour of trial, determine to build your spirit so that you may remain alert and prayerful.

Our leaders are calling for us. They are looking for someone who will commit to the long-term. There are pastors and leaders who are weary in the fight because we have not taken our place. We must take our place as God appointed armorbearers, assistants, and helpers in His army. God will hold us accountable for the support that should have been given if that leader fails because of it.

Daily Life

Have you ever had an overwhelmingly trouble-filled day, where circumstances seem to be against you on all sides? Look in on young Prince Jonathan (son of King Saul) on just that kind of day. It is a known fact his boss who was his father had backslidden from God. His dad had counted only 600 soldiers left from his 3,000-member army. He had just gotten the news that three war parties were dispatched from the enemies' camp. On top of those facts, the Philistines had banned blacksmiths in the land of Israel. Therefore, there was not a single sword or spear in the entire army of Israel that day, except his own and his father's. A day or so later, Prince Jonathan decided to go over to the enemy's camp with his armorbearer to spy out the camp. He did not tell anyone where they were going. They crossed a narrow pass between two steep cliffs. Upon arriving, he said to his armorbearer, "Let's go over to those heathen, maybe the Lord will do a miracle. It doesn't matter to him how many is in their army." His armorbearer said, "Yes! Do whatever is in your mind. I am with you heart and soul." The rest is history. Prince Jonathan and his armorbearer climbed over the cliff and killed about twenty men who fell left and right. After that, panic struck the entire Philistine army and at that same moment, a great earthquake came. The Philistines began killing each other in confusion. The Lord saved Israel that day through a man of God and his armorbearer.[14]

QUESTIONS FOR THOUGHT

---

1. Whose support is God holding you accountable?

2. Have you determined to develop what God has entrusted to you?

3. Has your courage and support bolstered your leader's confidence to obey God?

   VEry Good question ?!. DO I Give Him The sorport To Boost His confidere to obey God

10

THE MINISTRY OF AN ARMORBEARER

o o o o o o o o o o o o o o o o o o o o o o o o o o o o o o

Each one should use whatever gift he has received to serve others, faithfully administering God's grace in its various forms. If anyone serves, he should do it with the strength God provides, so that in all things God may be praised through Jesus Christ.

——1 Peter 4:11-12

N ow that the armorbearer's place and function has been established as an administration of helps. I would like to address some of the ministry functions in the Body of Christ. There is a need for more people clearly functioning in the ministry of helps and more specifically as an armorbearer. The main ministry functions of an armorbearer include being an assistant, intercessor, and a helper in the battle with their leader.

Look with me at an illustration that possibly reflects the general attitude of the Church toward a position of helps. Consider that Father God looks throughout the land (your Church) for a heart fully committed to him to use in ministry? He is developing His apostles, prophets, teachers, evangelists, and His pastors. Now, He is looking for His ministers called to help. He has looked, prompted, and called. Nevertheless, very few seem to take Him serious. "Nah! God wouldn't be calling me to be a helper," they say, "Is it a worthy calling to only assist the leader?" I believe it is. Jesus told us that if we as His representatives only give a glass of water to a disciple of his, we would receive a disciple's reward.[1]

Referring to the illustration above, I am cautious with speaking for God, yet I believe He is looking for men and women that will take the call to help seriously. When we do not take our Father's call seriously, we mistakenly think we are not being held accountable. <u>We show up any time we feel like it. When we do not feel like it, we don't. We do not make timeliness a priority. We quit helping without asking God what He thinks.</u> Woo! Let me move on before you put the book down.

Pattern Your Service

In Old Testament days, God appointed Bezalel, grandson of Hur, and filled him with the Spirit of God, giving him great wisdom, ability, and skill in constructing the Tabernacle and everything in it. *Alongside him, he appointed to help him Oholiab, son of Ahisamach.* Moses later revealed that God had gifted Beazalel and Oholiab to teach others their skills. Moses called a meeting and told the people to bring their offerings to God to build the Tabernacle. *The Spirit of God stirred the people.* Some brought materials and others supplied their time and their skills to the building of the Tabernacle. Soon, more than enough materials were gathered, and then Moses told Bezalel, Oholiab, and *all others who felt called to begin work.* When it was finished, they brought the tabernacle to Moses. Moses inspected their work and blessed the Israelites for they had done just as the Lord had commanded. Each person heard the call for his or her place of service. God then blessed them as a people for a job well done because of their unity and each individual serving where God called them. I pray that our hearts would be stirred for each to take the place God has called him to in the sanctuary, the true tabernacle set up by the Lord, not by man.[2]

Things Worth Remembering

Do you believe your service, as an armorbearer is a part of the ministry of Jesus? If not, change your mindset and acknowledge God has appointed you to support your leader in excellence. The writer of Revelation says, "Keep your clothes with you, that you may not be found naked and ashamed when our Lord comes." In other words, when our Master comes, may he find us doing what He's commanded us to do. May he come quickly in the midst of our intercession for His leaders. May the Bridegroom come and find us watching. Will our Lord arrive the second time and readily say, "Well done, my good and faithful servants?" Take a closer look with me at some of the ministry functions that we as armorbearers are called to be busy doing:

GOD'S APPOINTED ASSISTANT

> *Then the Lord said to Moses, "See, I have chosen Bezalel son of Uri, the son of Hur…And I have appointed Oholiab son of Ahisamach, of the tribe of Dan to assist him."*
> —— Exodus 31:1, 6

I overheard a slightly frustrated pastor saying, "I wish my assistant could help me in protecting my designated time to study. I know she means well, but when I go into my office to study because I'm teaching that night, I need the uninterrupted time. Even when I tell her I don't want to be interrupted, it's like I've mouthed the words with no meaning. She still allows people to enter and even ushers them in to me." She went on to say, "I wish I could give her a different mindset."

There is a different mindset to offer. There is the ministry of assisting instead of being just a good assistant, paid, or non-paid. Is there a difference? Yes. A God-appointed assistant who recognizes his or her higher calling will begin to minister to their leader with a different mindset.

- *Gain the mindset of an armorbearer.* You are a God-appointed assistant called to support the man or woman of God. Begin to look at your assistantship as ministry unto the Lord.

- *Protect or facilitate your leaders' time.* In the book of Acts, Stephen and Phillip were among the seven assigned to take care of the details of ministry while the Apostles ministered before the Lord.

- *Discern your leader's spirit.* Sometimes your officer is operating in their God-ordained office under the anointing and other times they are just being themselves. Respect them in either. When it's time to relax with your leader, be a good friend and relax. When it's time to take care of the Father's business and His people, slip back into the working mode with them.

- *Guard against familiarity.* Familiarity will affect how others look at your leader. If you are being too familiar at inappropriate times, it will cause respect for your leader to drain. Remain respectful of authority.

- *Be a gracious representative.* Know that in your serving, you are representing God and your officer. If you have to defer someone to protect your leaders' time, (as in the example given above), be gracious. You can be gentle but firm with God's sheep.

- *Be one of their strongest allies.* Show that you are always for them. In word and action, support your authority. If you discover criticism in others, work to show the good side or intention of your leader's heart.

If you haven't considered your assistantship as ministry in a while, or perhaps ever, surprise your leader, begin to handle things differently, take on the attitude of a minister of helps. Let your assisting become the ministry of assisting.

INTERCESSIONS OF AN ARMORBEARER

And I sought for a man among them that should make up the hedge, and stand in the gap before me for the land.

—— Ezekiel 22:30a

A description of an intercessor is one called to take the place of another, to stand in the gap, or as one of our pastors said, "Stand in the way." She says an evil spirit said to her as she interceded for our Senior Pastor's wife, "She's in the way, I can't get to her husband because she's always praying for him." Yes, God called us to be in the way of the enemy's plan for our leader's demise. As we pray, we are often able to stop the plans of the enemy or at least scatter his efforts. God somehow multiplies the odds when we pray for our leaders. Remember, one will put a thousand to flight and two will make ten thousand flee.

In operating as an armorbearer one must develop the characteristics of an intercessor. As a part of the divine call to minister in helps, comes a divine call to intercede for our leaders.[3] Allow the Holy Spirit to develop in you the heart of intercession. As an intercessor, one must possess:

- *Willingness.* The intercessor must be willing to pray when the Holy Spirit asks.

- *Obedience.* God's intercessors will be faithful to follow through on the promptings to pray for our leaders.

- *Confidentiality.* Can God trust you with the inner chambers of His house (the Church)? He may show you confidential things to pray about your leader. One operating in the true spirit of armorbearing can be trusted to pray for his leader in confidential matters.

- *Perseverance.* Do you pray until you get a release to stop? Do not give up on God's leader; He is not through with her or him either.

Pray until the victory comes! The Holy Spirit is faithful to let you know.

Are you involved in intercession for your leader? Good! Do not let our Father God have to look beyond you to find a faithful intercessor for your leader. Be the man or woman standing in the gap and making up the hedge for God's leader.

HELPERS IN THE BATTLE

These are they that came to David to Ziklag, while he yet concealed himself because of Saul the son of Kish; they were among the mighty men, his helpers in War.
— 1 Chronicles 12:1

I believe many of the same principles apply to spiritual warfare as natural warfare. I have been asked by one of my milder friends of faith, "Why are you so militant in your faith, Earma? I prefer a quiet church service with quiet prayers, not so much celebration, and noise." Without hesitation I responded, "I respect your beliefs, but I have learned if you are a human being you are in the war of good and evil. I know there is a God and He is a good God. On the other hand, I know there is a devil and he's a bad devil. Especially if you are a Christian, the devil treats you as if you are a threat to his kingdom. If you are a praying Christian, whether you know it or not, you are a threat to the devil's kingdom. I realize while we sing, whether it is quiet or loud, our enemy, the devil, has launched military strategies against the success of our life. In the same breath, I must assert that Jesus has already paid the price for the world by His death on the cross. And with all my strength, I enforce that victory in my life and others through prayer."

David's mighty men offer a good example of armorbearers being helpers in the war. The descriptions given in Scripture of David's mighty men will give us insight to the qualities God is building in His mighty men and women in New Testament days. Go with me to First Chronicles 12:1-40 and review some of the descriptions given to describe the helpers.[4] Verse 8 describes the Gadites who came over to help as:

- *Valiant* (brave warriors). The writer of Hebrews describes our strength as small in the day of battle if we faint. It has helped me tremendously in my faith to remember the words of Joyce Meyers, one of the mothers of practical faith, "If you are afraid, do it afraid. Just obey God."

- *Ready* (trained for war). Are you allowing Father God to discipline (train) or ready you? When Moses started out with the Israelites, they were not that far from the Promised Land. However, knowing the newly released slaves were not ready for battle, God took them through a longer route through the wilderness. He wanted to purge them, care for them, and simply prepare them for the victories that lay ahead. As biblical history tells us, the Israelites complained, disobeyed, and resisted their God into a judgment that lasted 40 years. Which brings us back to my original question rephrased, "Are you allowing Father God to lead you through the longer routes in life to ready you for your victories?"

- *Able* (skillful in handling shield and spear). Scripture tells us that the Gadite men were skilled, experienced, and even talented with handling their weapons of war. As a new Christian, I often dreamed of myself fighting our enemy the devil with brooms, sticks, dull knives or anything ineffective. Finally, I got tired of being beat up in life and my dreams, which I'm sure you've recognized was only a symbolic mirror of what was happening in my life. My Lord began to train me with our weapons that are not carnal (fleshly and ineffective), but mighty to the pulling down of the enemy's strongholds. He constantly walked me through Ephesians 6 until when I would receive a flashback of my battles I would see myself welding the shield of faith and skillfully using the sword (the Word of God), cutting the enemy's head off and ripping him to pieces. The writer of

Ephesians encourages us to be strong (able, skillful, effective) in the Lord and in His mighty power. As we stand against the schemes of the devil for our lives and our leader's life, he further instructs us to put on the full armor of God.

- *Leaders* (the least was match for a hundred and the greatest for a thousand). I believe the captain warriors of Gadite had entered into God's multiplication of power. No wonder the enemy fights our unity in marriages, families, holy partnerships and ultimately the Body of Christ. He knows what happens to his kingdom every time faith is exercised in the God that multiplies the odds against him. Look at some of the biblical examples of this divine phenomenon: Gideon and his greatly reduced army (300) defeated an uncounted number of men.[5] Jonathan and his armorbearer defeated several war parties and an army of men. Jesus fed approximately 10,000 people with two loaves and five fish. Prophet Isaiah said, "One would cause a thousand to flee and two would put 10,000 to flight." Take the lead in God's great army knowing that the God we serve multiplies our odds against the enemy.

- *Fierce* (face of a lion). Have you seen Reggie White's game-face (attitude), as he looks at the opposing team? There is no doubt in the opposing team's mind that they are about to get steam-rolled, if possible. In a similar way, we are to wear the face (attitude) of the lion towards our enemy. A number of the defining terms of fierce are bold, intense, and violent. These words confirm what our attitude should be in faith toward the devil's intrusion in our lives and our leader's life.

- *Swift* (gazelle on the mountain). Earlier in this book, we spoke briefly of maintaining a sense of urgency in developing the spirit of armorbearing. I believe our God wants this quality developed in His servants more. He wants us to remember the time is short. Jesus imparting the sense of urgency to His disciples said, "All of us must quickly (swiftly) carry out the tasks assigned us by the one who sent Me, for there is little time left before the night falls and all work comes to an end." [6] In light of this, let us be like gazelles upon the mountain in carrying out our assignments before God.

Ministry of Armorbearing Cultivated

To grow in your ministry, decide to periodically examine yourself and your actions. Am I faithful in interceding? Am I watchful in spirit? Does my Lord consider me a good ambassador of Him as well as my leader? I even examine why I am doing what I do. Maybe you do too. It is good for us to examine ourselves in this area. Each time I do this, I remember my ministry is as 'unto my Lord'. To continue to develop and grow in the ministry of an armorbearer, remember to do these things:

- *Take your place seriously.* Others will follow suit. Often we don't gain the respect we deserve because we have not learned to respect our place in ministry.

- *Be a faithful intercessor for your leader.* Make the choice to be faithful to God by being faithful in your calling to intercede. Stand in the gap for your assigned leader until the victory comes.

- *Maintain a watchful spirit.* Be a watchman on the wall. Remain ready and willing to assist. The servants who the master left in charge started out good, but when it took a long time for their master to return, they got lazy, started partying and beating the other servants...[7]

- *Determine to be a good ambassador.* Remember you represent Christ and your authority. Represent them well. Maintain a gracious spirit, seeking to uphold the attributes of love.[8]

- *Stay in the battle.* As armorbearers, we battle with and for our leaders. Hold up your leader's arms when it counts.

There is no substitute for a person who knows what he or she has been called by God to do. The support ministries need the focus and intensity you bring to your uniquely formed position as an armorbearer.

Daily Life

David who started out in the king's service as a faithful armorbearer almost twenty years earlier, now stood ready to possess God's promise that he would be king. Nevertheless, he needed support to do it. Men and groups of men began to come from all over the land to support David, not just any men, but men already proven in character, courage, and valor came to his side. They came not with complacent attitudes, but as men who understood the times and knew what God called them to do. They were fully armed and very loyal to David. All these men were volunteers and understood authority. There was such an array of men with a single purpose in mind of making David, king of Israel, that all of Israel became ready for the change. Men had joined his army almost every day until he had a tremendous army—the army of God. David became king instead of Saul, just as the Lord said would happen.[9]

QUESTIONS FOR THOUGHT

---

1. Do you consider your position of armorbearing a commission?

2. Have you committed to pray the prayer of intercession for your leader?

3. Has God stirred you to action lately?

11

DEVELOPING THE
CHARACTER OF CHRIST

o o o o o o o o o o o o o o o o o o o o o o o o o o o o o o o o

And even though Jesus was God's Son, He had to learn from experience what it was like to obey, when obeying meant problems and difficulties.

——Hebrews 5:8 TLB

Have you noticed that much of how we respond to life's circumstances has to do with our character? God desires to build character within us. He desires to train (discipline) us as His children.[1] Training and disciplining does not always feel good. In fact, it can be downright painful. Ask any private in a military boot camp or any professional athlete during his training season. The Apostle Paul encouraged us about God's training, "No discipline seems pleasant at the time, but painful. Later on, however, it produces a harvest of righteousness and peace for those who have been trained by it." [2]

Often throughout Scripture we find God saying to man...I wanted to know what was in your heart. I tested you to know if you would keep My commands. After Abraham's character test, God said, "Now I know that you love Me." To the Israelites He said, "I tested you in the wilderness so that I would know what you would do." [3] As with any test, the day or season of the test is not the time to develop and prepare. Therefore, I believe the time to cooperate with God to build character is the now—everyday. In the everyday processes of life, we have opportunity to develop character (moral strength). Choices create character.

Problems and adversity give us opportunity to develop character. The Apostle Paul (as incredible as it may sound) in one of his letters to the Roman church, encouraged them to rejoice when facing difficulties, "We can rejoice, too, when we run into problems and trials for we know that they are good for us—they help us learn to be patient. And patience develops strength of character in us and helps us trust God more each time we use it until finally, our hope and faith are strong and steady." [4] We develop character every time we make a right choice. John C. Maxwell, America's expert on leadership and successful executive says, "We create it (character) every time we make choices—to cop out or dig out of a hard situation, to bend the truth or stand under the weight of it, to take the easy money or pay the price." [5] By daily recognizing, developing, and refining the moral strength in us, we are co-laborers in building the character God desires to see in His children.

Pattern Your Service

Little Samuel was helping the Lord by assisting Eli. In fact, his mother, Hannah, had consecrated him for service in the house of God since before birth. The man of God, Eli, and his sons showed a lack of character. The times were dark for God's people and character seemed to be lacking in most. Yet the scripture tells us Samuel grew in favor with God and with man to the point that God let none of his words fall to the ground void. The apostle James told us, "The man who claims to be religious and yet, does not bridle his tongue is not as he claims to be." We can pattern our service after the young Samuel who grew in favor with God and man by developing character. He left us a certain example of being the Lord's helper by serving Eli. His words matched his actions so much that God could always perform His will and word through Samuel.[6]

Things Worth Remembering

Allow Father God to develop character in you through the ministry of assisting. Character is vital to our ability to carry the anointing God has for His army. The world's nations can fall and rise based on the character of its leaders. Just as much and more, our leaders in the Kingdom of God are operating with the character built in their season of serving. When you choose humility instead of what others think, you should know that in your ministry of service you are building moral strength. Each time you walk in love instead of retaliation or revenge, I assure you your character has grown. Choosing patience with the will of God instead of doing it your own way will build the strong faith you desire. Cooperate with God as He endeavors to build character in you through your armorbearing.

People without inner strength cannot be counted on day after day because their ability to perform changes constantly. If people do not know what to expect from you, at some point they lose faith in you. Character inspires several things in the people around us. Character inspires:

- *Consistency.* Billy Graham is a man that communicates consistency in our modern world. In his life, he has consistently shown humility, compassion, and godly integrity. From the White House to the street, people have observed his consistent godly living and compassion for lost souls. Your consistency will inspire hope and faith in a world that sees so little.

- *Trust.* Psychologists agree that we earn trust. Which is why most people do not give their trust to just anyone. A pastor friend of mine said, "I trust people until they give me a reason not to." I responded with, "That's wonderful, but I don't trust until a person gives me a reason to trust them." Whatever your struggle, your character will inspire trust in those around you.

- *Favor.* Remember Prophet Samuel grew in favor with man and God because of his character. In addition, Jesus, our chief example, grew in favor with God and with man. My former jail ministry leader used to admonish us to follow the rules of the authorities of each prison facility because of the favor involved. Our adherence to the rules built an atmosphere where the officials and attendants favored us and wanted to cooperate. The integrity and character of the ministry team built trust and respect. Grow in favor with God and man because you submit to the authorities in your life.

We need character in our ministers and in our leaders of the faith. We need character developed in our servants of the house. If God has appointed you to walk as an armorbearer to one of our leaders, know that character can be developed through this position. David's mighty men again offer us exemplary qualities that will support God's anointing.

The writer of Chronicles describes the gathering of God's Old Testament army, "For at that time day by day men kept coming to David to help him, until there was a great army, like the army of God"[7] In the same way, I see men and women all over the Body of Christ saying, Aha! This is my time. This is my appointed place until the Body of Christ will be the great army of God in which He has called us to be in these last days. The same character that was noted in David's mighty men will be developed in us as we each take our place in God's army today. Listed below are other commendable qualities mentioned by the writer of Chronicles in verses 32 and 38:

- *Understanding* (understood the times). These men understood the season and the time in which they lived. Jesus rebuked the Pharisees' unbelief in His day saying, "You see and understand the changes of the weather by the clouds or the sun shining brightly with no clouds. Yet you refuse to look and understand the times you are living in." Join me as we determine to be like David's mighty men in believing and discerning the times (last days) in which we live.

- *Wisdom* (knew what to do). The mighty men of David were wise and knew what to do. Let us be wise and discerning in knowing what to do in the Body of Christ. Find your place and do what God has called you to do. Be the men and women of purpose that the Father God has said we are.

- *Loyalty* (single-minded, fully determined). Are you fully determined in your place of service? Only then can we be single-minded and loyal to our leaders. The Apostle Paul gave us wisdom about maintaining the mindset of a soldier when fulfilling loyalty during difficult seasons, "Endure hardship with us like a good soldier of Christ Jesus." [8] Decide with me to be loyal and serve single-mindedly as God's great armorbearers.

- *Volunteerism* (could keep rank, good follower). Good soldiers have no problem with keeping rank. They know their designated spot and follow in place. If we as God's army of volunteers would apply the same principle, we would not break rank but follow our leaders as they follow Christ.

- *Unity* (of one mind and purpose). God knew the power of unity and working in one purpose when He confused the people building the tower of Babel. Just as Satan knows the power we would exercise as one in Christ, he strives to create confusion and division in our midst. Pray with me for the unity of the Body of Christ, as our Lord prayed for the unity of His followers that we might accomplish His will.

Once more, I must say it seems our Father God is painstakingly involved in working character in us. However, it is up to us to work together with him so that we may reap the harvest of righteousness he longs to give to us.

Character Cultivated

We desire people of character in our churches, our cities, our countries, and our world. Most if not all of the success stories turned failures in recent years, have been partially due to lack of character. No one can rise above the limitations of his character. Billy Graham was asked to comment on how he was able to maintain character in the face of so many ministry leaders showing a lack of character. He responded with, "People have put me on too high a pedestal. We do the same with other leaders. I know, however, I am not as good as some people think I am. I have seen men in the depths of wickedness and have thought to myself, 'There I go, except by the grace of God.' I have to depend on God every day to help me live as I should." We also must depend on the grace of God to help us live, as we should. To develop character in your life on a daily basis:

- *Make right choices.* Remember character is a choice. Invite God in on your choices. You will find it makes a lifetime of difference.

- *Recognize your character will preach the gospel.* Determine to set a good example for those watching your witness.

- *Remember bad company corrupts good character.* Watch the company you keep. Are they a good influence upon your life or a bad one?

- *Depend on the grace of God.* When you make a mistake, repent, and begin again. My pastor, Mike Hayes says, "God is a God of new beginnings. Look at how He provides us an opportunity for a fresh start each new season, New Year, new month, new week, and every fresh morning."

We have determined that choices create character. If you have been unfortunate to make quite a few wrong choices in life as I have, then this will be good news to you. Pastor Amy Hossler encouraged me saying, "Even a wrong or bad choice repented of can eventually build good character." Our Father God has promised (if we ask for it) to forgive us and cleanse us of all unrighteousness. Additionally, He promised to work all things to our good.[9]

Daily Life

Recently, an actor with a career spanning over half a century told of his humble beginnings and one of his character choices that changed his life forever, "I was newly married and a new father. We were barely making it; living off my waiting tables and doing a few acting jobs here and there. A man called one day offering an assignment paying a lot of money (back then) to play a young rebellious man spewing out obscenities to his father. After thinking of the disrespect it would bring to my father, a good man, I turned it down and declared I would only play roles in which my family could be proud. Almost a month later, the man called back with a respectable role and an offer to represent me as my agent. He said he could not stop thinking about me. He said, 'If a man feeding his family off pennies could turn down an assignment offering this much money, there had to be something to him.' He represented me as my agent for 30 years until his death. The role he offered me was *Guess Who's Coming to Dinner?*" That actor was *Sidney Poitier,* who went on to win for his work in the movie, *Lilies of the Field,* 1963; the only Oscar for Best Actor awarded to an African-American in a 40 year span of U.S. history. Mr. Poitier's choice during that difficult time changed the course of his life.

QUESTIONS FOR THOUGHT

1. Have you realized you are the Lord's helper if you are assisting your appointed leader?

2. What character quality do you believe God is working in you now and are you cooperating?

3. Has God desired to know what you would do through a difficult choice?

12

BEING AN ANTICIPATOR

○ ○
And it shall come to pass, before they call I will answer; while they are still speaking I will hear.

——Isaiah 65:24

When you ask God to teach you to do something, I have learned to prepare for a different thought pattern. After all, His ways are not our ways and His thoughts are not our thoughts. The good news is they can be. Anytime we ask for God's wisdom, His understanding or His perspective He is faithful to give it to us. The writer of James says, He will give it to us liberally without making us feel ashamed that we asked.[1]

Earlier, in chapter nine, I mentioned that I asked the Holy Spirit to show me how to be an effective armorbearer. The kind that walks worthy of his or her calling. At the time I received this teaching, I was talking to the Lord more about my needs and desires. I asked Him about a particular need of mine and He responded by pointing to my leader's needs. He began to show me how to anticipate those of my leader. Why is this important? I believe because He promised, "Before they call I will answer..."[2] We can be excited and honored that God would use us as a tool to fulfill His promise!

Needs are inevitable, we all have them. However, a good servant can anticipate those of his leader. Study your leader and begin to know them. Holy Spirit-guided observation will begin to point to what they need before they sometimes express it.

Pattern Your Service

It was an important dinner held in the honor of Jesus at the home of special friends. Jesus would come out of the city Jerusalem to visit this home, leaving the plots and plans of His enemies behind for a few hours, knowing that His day of trials was almost upon Him. He lounged at the table with Lazarus, the man he had raised from the dead. Martha was busy serving. *Mary* (Martha and Lazarus' sister) took nard (perfume) worth a year of wages and anointed Jesus. The fragrance filled the whole house. As it is with all true service and worship, it moves people. One may be moved with compassion or another with criticism when observing a true servant. In the case of Jesus', team treasurer, he left no doubt in anyone's mind which emotion he yielded to after sharply criticizing them for allowing such a waste of funds that could have gone to the poor. Jesus, knowing the motives of Judas's heart, rebuked him saying, "Leave her alone she is the only one that has anticipated my need for anointing before burial (He had told his followers on several occasions of His death in a few days). As a memorial of this act, she will always be mentioned in the gospel." Mary offers us a beautiful example of service that has anticipated her leader's need. With the help of the Holy Spirit, we can worship our God by anticipating the need of our appointed leader.[3]

Things Worth Remembering

To anticipate the needs of your leader, you must first be attentive and a good listener with the Holy Spirit. To be attentive to the Holy Spirit, you are called to be willing, prayerful, ready and quiet in spirit.

- *Willing.* Are you willing to anticipate another's need? A part of anticipation includes laying your needs aside to attend to another.

You may be praying for your leaders while your needs seemingly go unmet. Not so. God takes care of the faithful.

- *Prayerful.* Prayer prepares your spirit to hear God. Remain prayerful and walk in the Spirit.

- *Ready.* Stay ready for the Holy Spirit to prompt you. If you get distracted or have to stop to do something else, you will miss the time of anticipation.

- *Quiet.* Remaining quiet in spirit is not always easy for talkative or quiet personalities. Your task may be taming your tongue in your mouth or putting a harness on the thoughts in your mind. Either way, if you are always talking you may miss the Holy Spirit's directions. Sssh!

Anticipation Cultivated

In God's kingdom, to increase something, you usually decrease. Jesus instructed us in this matter with, "Whoever finds his life will lose it, and whoever loses his life for My sake will find it." [4] To grow in anticipation in your serving, you must decrease:

- *Be willing.* Allow God to give you his instructions of anticipated serving. In part one of this book, we discussed how God's view of servanthood is quite different from the way our society looks at it. If needed, allow Him to change or expand your thinking. My husband and my first set of personal instructions from God included a question, "How willing are you to give a 100% in service?" The Holy Spirit instructed us to stay with our appointed leaders from start to finish of their ministry time. Our commitment did not allow us to leave them ministering in the building while we went home. We realized that just as we walked out the door, often a need would arise.

- *Be flexible.* To increase in anticipation, one must be ready for the unexpected timing of details. Flexibility will keep you ready for the unexpected in serving. How ready are you to change your plans to accommodate your leader's need? Are you prompt to obey the Holy Spirit when he wakes you to pray for that unforeseen problem that the enemy has planned against your ministry and leader? Allow anticipation to grow in you by being flexible.

- *Travel light.* In traveling the narrow path of an anticipating servant, we must put away unnecessary baggage. There is no room to carry it. My heavenly Father gave me a vision of my arrival in a very spacious place of service after traveling down a narrow path. I observed some people coming down the same path after me. When they came through, they said, "Whew! That was narrow; I could not bring any baggage with me. I had to put it all down to walk." What baggage, you may ask? Pride would be baggage. Selfishness and offenses could be baggage. To be an anticipator of needs, you must develop an unselfish and humble attitude not being touchy, fretful or quick to anger.[5]

- *Remain teachable.* Be led by the Holy Spirit. There is no substitute for the Holy Spirit's guidance and counsel. Even if I have thought I knew most things about what I was doing, I have never failed to gain a fresh perspective when I include the Holy Spirit. As with all things that are important to do well, I simply say, "Holy Spirit teach me…" He has promised to guide and teach us in the way we should go.[6]

- *Develop prudence.* One that anticipates will develop the ability to look ahead and serve in expectancy. The proverbial writer instructs us with, "A prudent man is sensible; he watches for problems and difficulties and prepares to meet them. The simpleton never looks, and suffers the consequences."[7]

Daily Life

My husband and I have been frequenting a restaurant for about ten years. We love the food and service we receive there. Over the years, it has been consistently good. One of the waitresses has become a special friend of ours. We call her Sunshine. When we walk in the door, Sunshine ladles us a hot bowl of our favorite soup and serves our drinks. She discerns whether we want the same thing or we might want something different that day. If she thinks we want the same thing, she puts the order in right after serving the soup. I am assuming it's written on our face if we want something different, because she will ask. Somehow, she has gotten it right 99% of the time. You could say we are just highly predictable people. That is partly true, but I think the other part is she anticipates our desires. Sunshine, as well as other good servers, offers us an excellent pattern of anticipating.

QUESTIONS FOR THOUGHT

---

1. Are your actions of service fragrant with worship of your God?

2. Do you consider yourself as an instrument of the Lord?

3. What must you put down, take off or put away to walk the narrow path of servanthood?

13

THE GEHAZI FACTOR

Gehazi, the servant of Elisha the man of God, said to himself,
"My master was too easy on Naaman, this Aramean, by not
accepting from him what he brought. As surely as the Lord lives,
I will run after him and get something from him."

——*2 Kings 5:20 NIV*

I have discovered all Scripture is useful for instruction and example. Our Bible does not hold back in showing us examples of what not to do.[1] In this chapter, we are going to look at some examples of wrong choices and disobedience in Scripture. It is a fact that some will not choose a walk of obedience. Not everyone will continue in faith as they serve God. I am always saddened when I see someone receive the call, serve enthusiastically, and for whatever reason quit. Some give up because they get weary. Others give up because they have no root in themselves. I have observed all kinds of reasons why people give up, realizing except by the grace of God; I may have given up in the valley of decision. Join me as I look at some things not to do in serving as God's armorbearer.

Pattern Your Service

The young man, Gehazi, started out as an obedient assistant to Elisha the prophet. However, later he succumbed to the temptation of covetousness and familiarity. When Naaman, a foreigner, who God healed through Elisha's ministry, offered gifts, the man of God refused the reward lest it be thought a foreigner could come and buy a miracle from the God of Israel. Gehazi, thinking to himself that his master had been too easy on the foreigner, ran after him to see what he could get. He lied to Naaman, received $4,000 and two suits of clothing, returned home and hid the gifts. When he returned to work, Elisha confronted him. Because of Gehazi's attitude and disobedience, the leprosy that Naaman was healed of came on him and his descendants. Gehazi's familiarity and covetousness resulted in the loss of his respect and reverence for the office of prophet. This story offers an example of what not to do in serving your leader.[2]

Things Worth Remembering

When God has called you to be an armorbearer or anything else, your faith will be tested. The question will be asked, "Are you really called by God?" Circumstances will pose the question, "Will you continue?" Satan and his imps have designed circumstances to take us off course. Here are a few things to guard against as we endeavor to stay on God's course of servanthood:

- *Guard against the spirit of familiarity.* You can become so familiar in relationship that you lose your reverence and respect for the office in which your leader serves. David never lost the reverence for the ordained office of kingship. Even when his king no longer deserved respect, he continued to respect God's man and his office.

- *Don't confuse what belongs to your leader as belonging to you.* Many times as servants of the Lord, we begin to realize we are chosen vessels of His. With this realization may come the opportunity to become confused about what belongs to us. The enemy's bait becomes, "You have worked so closely with your leader, you can do better than him or her. God called you, too. He speaks to you…" I encourage you to remember where God placed you. Remain there until God moves you. Miriam, sister to Moses, fell for this dangerous thought pattern. She began to complain with her brother Aaron, "Doesn't God speak to us, also?" She received leprosy because of her sins of insubordination and criticism. Her brother, Moses, prayed and she received her healing.

- *Determine to be yourself.* It is wise to be obedient and agreeable. It is not wise to lose your personality and become false. Remain unpretentious in your relationships. Allow your leader to be himself or herself, but never pretend.

- *Acknowledge relationship boundaries.* There are normal boundaries that are set by what kind of relationship you enjoy with your leader. For example, if you had a predecessor in serving your appointed leader, allow time to get to know each other. Do not try to be that person to them.

- *Avoid competition.* Do not compete with your leader's family, ministry associates or other close associates. When I learned that we each have a place in God's kingdom and in the ministry, I ceased to strive for a position. I began to know and fulfill my place and my function as a minister.

Obedience Cultivated

Jesus said to His disciples, "If you love Me, you will obey Me." Here are a few things listed below that will encourage obedience in your life with God and as an armorbearer:

- *Wear humility as a garment.* Resist pride. We may choose the garment of humility for the Apostle Peter instructed us with, "Humble yourselves, therefore, under God's mighty hand, that he may lift you up in due time." [3]

- *Seek love, the highest of all gifts.* Love will cover a multitude of wrongs. Resist the bait of Satan. Jesus said, "Offenses will come. But woe to those it comes through." We again have a choice. We can choose to obey God and forgive rather than listen to Satan, who designs offenses to get us to hold a grudge and get so far off course we never make it back.

- *Guard against criticism of your leader.* Badmouthing your leader will place you in sin and open the door for the enemy's infiltration in your life. Miriam's criticism of her leader did not open the door for a blessing, but a curse. Gehazi's critical remarks led to further disobedience and later judgment.

- *Walk by the Spirit.* Resist complacency. Seek to stay zealous. It is man's sinful nature to lean toward laziness, pride, provoking, and envying one another. However, the spirit man's desire is to obey God.[4] Jesus warned his disciples, "Watch and pray, the spirit (man) is willing but the flesh (natural man) is weak." We must remain alert for our enemy the devil prowls around like a lion to see whom he may devour.[5]

- *Make a commitment to act.* Many times, we fall into disobedience because we have not committed to hear the Word of God and act. The writer of James commanded us to, "Be doers of the Word and not just hearers."

Daily Life

Jesus chose a donkey called Sam for a special task. He was consecrated (prepared and set apart). Jesus sent two of His disciples to tell Sam's owner it was time; He had need of him. Jesus and Sam, the donkey, came into Jerusalem together on the day now known as Palm Sunday. Crowds gathered at the entrance of Jerusalem. They carried palm branches and cheered as Jesus rode in on Sam. Sam had been called into the ministry of helps. He was a special chosen vessel for this task of helping and supporting Jesus for His entry into Jerusalem. The crowd cheered and shouted more at each step they took. As they shouted, Sam began to think they were cheering for him. His chest swelled; lifting each hoof a little higher until he was marching, thinking to himself, "Oh! Listen at them cheer for me. I must be a great donkey for them to cheer for me like that." Somehow, Sam, the donkey, became confused thinking the praises and cheers were for him. Upon arrival at their destination, Jesus got off. Sam's task was complete. Suddenly it hit Sam, all the praise and honor belonged to the Lord. Jesus leaned over patting Sam's back and whispered, "Well done, my good and faithful servant." Sam's chest swelled a second time but for a different reason. He was honored and grateful that out of all the donkeys available, he was chosen for this special task. His eyes misted, as he was led away thinking, "He said to me, "Well done…"

QUESTIONS FOR THOUGHT

---

1. Have you been baited for offense lately?

2. Have you committed the sin of criticism of your authority?

3. Have you ever confused what belonged to your leader as yours?

14

DARING TO BE FAITHFUL

o o o o o o o o o o o o o o o o o o o o o o o o o o o o o o o

God is not unrighteous to forget your work and labour of love,
which you have shown toward His name.

——*Hebrews 6:10*

Ll over the world churches, businesses, and organizations are looking for faithful people, people that will sign up for the long-term.
The number of faithful seems to drop to lower and lower amounts. As
time passes, the numbers of marriages remaining faithful are fewer.
People are known to have two and three careers in a lifetime, as
opposed to the twenty and thirty year tenures. Much of this has to do
with the changing climate of our society. My opinion is the abounding
sin in our nation and world today has an even greater impact. Yet,
there's hope for this bleak picture, the writer of Romans says, where sin
abounds that much more does grace abound.[1] Furthermore, our
Father God has given us the ability and the command to be faithful.

Throughout part two of this book, I have spoken from my heart as
an armorbearer. I have sought to write down some of the lessons the
Holy Spirit has taught our Church family about armorbearing. In
chapter ten, *The Ministry of an Armorbearer*, we examined three of the
main ministry functions of an armorbearer. Our appointment as assistants, our intercessions, and fulfilling the role of helpers in the battle
came to the forefront. We gained insight on how the development of
character will strengthen the ability to carry the anointing in our lives

forever through chapter eleven's, *Developing the Character of Christ*. In chapter twelve's, *Being an Anticipator*, I laid my lessons before you from our teacher, the Holy Spirit, about anticipating our leader's needs. Through chapter thirteen, *The Gehazi Factor*, I felt warned all over again by the Scripture's counsel against disobedience. Those warnings included being on guard against the sins of the heart, aimed to take us off the path of service. Finally, in this chapter, I charge you with a dare to be faithful in your service to a faithful God.

Faithfulness can be considered as longevity. Faithfulness is staying for the long haul. Fulfilling our commitment accomplishes faithfulness. It takes courage to be faithful. It takes stamina to swim upstream when many are drifting downstream. God honors faithfulness in any service to Him. *Buddy Bell*, in his Ministry of Helps handbook says, "God called my faithfulness—my crowbar, and then commanded me to use it." [2] Our God is one who remembers the righteous and faithful to a thousand generations.

Pattern Your Service

Abraham was called God's friend, yet he was as completely human with similar passions as you or me. For example, out of fear he lied to a king about his wife, Sarah, being his sister. He almost destroyed a whole kingdom, when the King took Sarah for his own. In mercy, God showed the king what he had done wrong then he promptly let her go. Even with Abraham's human makeup and tendencies, God declared him faithful. Abraham showed he believed God by his obedience beyond his mistakes, shortcomings, and difficult choices. He was called faithful by what he continued to do as well as what he believed. God finally said of him, "I know him (Abraham); he is faithful. He will teach his children and all those with him how to be faithful. I can trust him to keep My ways and I will do all that I promised him." Abraham's example inspires us to be faithful in what we do in spite of our mistakes and shortcomings.[3]

Things Worth Remembering

God has promised blessings for the faithful. We can choose to be faithful. It is, one of the few things, we can offer our Lord. He has given us the gift of salvation and the gift of His Holy Spirit. It is His good pleasure to give us His kingdom. We can be faithful to Jesus and His ministry. Additionally, God remembers the faithful. Hebrew 6:10 encourages us with, "God is not unrighteous to forget your work and labor of love (faithfulness), which you have shown toward His name."
4 Here are a few promises in Scripture to remember about faithfulness:

- *To the faithful you show yourself faithful, to the blameless you show yourself blameless, to the pure you show yourself pure.* —Psa. 18:25

- *Love the Lord, all His saints! The Lord preserves the faithful.* —Psa. 31:23a

- *For He guards the lives of His faithful ones.* —Psa. 97:10b

- *You have been faithful with a few things; I will put you in charge of many things.* —Mt. 25:23b

Satan is an enemy to our faithfulness. He hates it when we are faithful. I think because it reflects a faithful God to a faithless world. Therefore, it is no surprise when he sets traps and distractions to draw us from our God-ordained path. In our case, he wants to divert us from our path of service. Beware of these baits and traps of Satan:

> *Offenses* are the bait of Satan to get one off the path of faithfulness in God. Faithfulness resists offenses. Satan will seek to trap you in unforgiveness toward a person. However, remember we always have a choice; we can be offended or forgive. Forgiveness is the right choice. Be alert to this trap because most people that have been trapped do not even realize it. Stay in tune with the Holy Spirit, for He will point out any baits of Satan making sure you are aware to make the right choice.

Pride can be very subtle in its diversion. I found myself listening to a woman confessing her discovery of pride in her life. She admitted to saying to her leader, "I have a degree in engineering and I am not going to continue in my volunteering in the Church if all you have for me to do is collating and copying." She later repented and continued faithfully helping wherever she was needed. When we are attentive to the Holy Spirit and careful to judge ourselves concerning pride, we will never be on the outside of the call and destiny God has planned for us.

Laziness and selfishness are twin enemies to the development of God's faithfulness in our life. Allowing negative emotions and feelings to dictate our behavior rather than commitment will result in laziness. "I don't feel like it tonight. My leader will just have to make it without me..." is a common and selfish train of thought. When our fleshly desires threaten to rise up and take control, we are to offer a living sacrifice of our bodies.[5] Then we will rise to the level of commitment we are called to as faithful servants of the most high God.

Impatience is a sure enemy to faithfulness. My friends who I mentioned in an earlier chapter grew weary of waiting for their appointed leader to acknowledge their gifts and talents. They felt they should have been recommended for leadership. They did not want to hear my advice of, "I'm sure it will happen in God's timing. You are excellent candidates for leadership..." They replied, "Posh! God already knows about us and we are giving our leader six months to recognize us; if not, we are out of here." Their leader did not, and they left. Later, they came back, admitted they were wrong, and should have waited. The writer of Hebrews encourages us with, "You have need of patience, and so after you have done the will of God you may receive his promise."[6]

Faithfulness Cultivated

God's faithfulness is our shield and rampart.[7] Yet, He has commanded His ministers (those entrusted with the secret things of God) to be faithful.[8] Jeremiah put it this way, "God is looking throughout the land to find someone with their heart fully committed to Him to show Himself strong on their behalf." Here are a few qualities that will nurture faithfulness in your life and ministry:

Develop loyalty—Form a covenant relationship with your leader. Doing so will create an allegiance that will move heaven and earth on behalf of others and yourselves.[9]

Perseverance—The storms of life will come to any ministry. The writer of Joshua describes a scene during Joshua's life and ministry. The people of God were wavering in their decision to serve God wholeheartedly. Joshua put a clear choice before them saying, "Choose this day whom you will serve. Choose life or death."[10] Determine like Joshua when tough times came to their ministry, "As for me and my house, we will serve the Lord."

Love much—Years ago, I was on my knees crying to my God because two good friends who started out faithful at the same time I did had backslidden in their Christianity. I was distraught because I wondered if they could go back, perhaps something could happen and I would go back to a life of sin. With tears, I said, "Lord, don't ever let me go, I love you so much…" He comforted me and gave me peace with these words, "Many have come, some will go, but you will stay." Let love be your reason for faithfulness.

Additionally, in talking with people who have managed to be faithful, they encouraged us with some practical tips:

- *A couple married over 40 years:* Keep a sense of humor in life. Laugh a lot at yourself and with others. If you make a mistake, pick yourself up, forgive, keep going, and keep laughing.

- *A man in the ministry over 50 years:* Serve God with all your heart. Doing this will build faithfulness in you. Realize the devil is a bad devil and God is a good God! This knowledge will make you want to be faithful. Knowing the devil brings captivity and God brings restoration will let you know we have to be faithful.

- *A couple in the ministry over 25 years:* Be responders, not reactors. Take it slow. If someone is rushing you and pressuring you to make a decision, it's probably not God. At the least, it's not His timing. The more we walk in God's timing, the more we will be faithful.

- *A woman who has lived over 80 years:* I learned not to take life so seriously. Have some fun along the way. God enjoys you better that way. He really does delight in you, so there's no reason to be faithless.

Daily Life

Impulsive yet faithful, focused yet sometimes double-minded, passionate but often presumptuous, all described an assistant of Jesus. When Jesus prophesied to His helpers and disciples that they would all forsake Him in His hour of trial, that young assistant, Peter, spoke the loudest, "Never! I will die with you, Lord!" Jesus, recognizing the passion and presumption in Peter, turned to him saying, "Peter, before the rooster crows the third time, you will have denied Me three times." It happened just as Jesus said it would. It's also recorded when Peter turned back, he strengthened his brothers. Peter continued through his failures to the fulfillment of his ministry. God counted him among the faithful.[11]

QUESTIONS FOR THOUGHT

---

1. Have you counted the cost of your ministry?

2. Does your faith statement include continue?

3. Has your loyalty passed any test?

15

TEN MORE POWER PRINCIPLES OF SERVING

o o o o o o o o o o o o o o o o o o o o o o o o o o o o o o
He who tends a fig tree will eat its fruit, and he who looks after his leader will be honored.

——*Pr. 27:18*

F ellow servants of Christ, my prayer has been that the Holy Spirit of God will have birthed, stirred, or even completed the spirit of your mind concerning armorbearing, as only He can do. My goal has been to present the subject matter in a concise manner, being respectful of the busy lives you lead. I aspired to construct a book where you could open it up and receive bite-size insightful encouragement in your faith as an armorbearer. In addition, when you have more time available, you could dive in and feast to strengthen your walk and service to the Lord.

Furthermore, my objective has been to offer honor and recognition where little has been offered to those who have already captured the spirit and heart of servanthood. I acknowledge many people have been walking in the spirit of armorbearing and servanthood long before I decided to sit down and write this book. My hat is off to you. Through your intensity and passion of serving our Lord through serving others, many of us have been provoked to do more. Now, join me in a short walk through ten more principles of serving.

1. *Serve with proven character*

   "The only thing that walks back from the tomb with the mourners and refuses to be buried is the character of a man. This is true. What a man is survives him. It can never be buried." *J.R. Miller*

   Patience produces proven character in us and helps us trust God more each time we use it until, finally, our hope and faith are strong and steady. *Romans 5:4*

2. *Serve accepted*

   "Turn no one away that wants to serve. Accept others as Christ has accepted you." *Kathy Hayes, Senior Pastor, Covenant Church*

   The one who comes to Me, I will never, never reject. *John 6:37b NKJV*

3. *Serve with greatness*

   "Everybody can be great...because anybody can serve. You don't have to have a college degree to serve. You don't have to make your subject and verb agree to serve. You only need a heart full of grace and a soul generated by love." *Martin L. King, Jr.*

   To be the greatest, be a servant. *Matthew 23:11*

4. *Serve as an example*

   "One example can make a difference." *Mike Hayes, Senior Pastor, Covenant Church*

   Be an example (pattern) for the believers, in speech, in conduct, in love, in faith, and in purity. *1 Timothy 4:12a*

5. *Serve for the glory of God*

"A great deal of good can be done in the world if one is not too careful who gets the credit." *Bill Cosby*

So then, whether you eat or drink, or whatever you may do, do all for the honor and glory (credit) of God. *1 Corinthians 10:31 Amp*

6. *Serve through love*

"People don't care how much you know, until they know how much you care…about them." *St. Francis Xavier*

Through love, serve one another. *Galatians 5:13*

7. *Serve as sowing a seed*

"A tree is known by its fruit; a man by his deeds. A good deed is never lost, he who sows courtesy reaps friendship, and he who plants kindness gathers love." *St. Basil 329-379, Bishop of Caesarean*

Do not be deceived: God cannot be mocked. A man reaps what he sows. *Galatians 6:7*

8. *Serve setting a higher standard for yourself*

"Hold yourself responsible for a higher standard than anybody else expects of you." *Henry Ward Beecher (1813-1887, American Preacher, Orator, Writer)*

Like a boxer, I buffet my body—handle it roughly, discipline it and subdue it, lest possibly after proclaiming to others the Gospel and things pertaining to it, I myself should become unfit—not stand the test and be unapproved—and rejected (as a counterfeit.) *1 Corinthians 9:27*

9. *Serve with a sense of urgency*

"When one door closes, another opens. Seize the opportunity while the path remains lit." *Unknown*

As long as it is day, we must do the work of him who sent me. Night is coming, when no one can work. *John 9:4*

10. *Serve loyally*

"The ultimate measure of a man is not where he stands in moments of comfort, but where he stands at times of challenge and controversy." *Martin Luther King, Jr.*

Whoever eats my flesh and drinks my blood remains in Me, and I in him...From that time many of His disciples went back, and walked no more with Him. Then said Jesus to the twelve, "Will ye also go away?" *John 6:56,66,67*

In part one of this book, I started with ten powerful principles of serving. As God developed me in this teaching, He gave me many more. I have discovered these may be applied to different aspects of life. With God's wisdom, His principles are multi-faceted and applicable to every servant's life. I bless and encourage you in your journey to becoming better servants of Christ through serving His leaders.

NOTES

Preface

1. See Exodus 4:14-17.

2. See 1 Corinthians 12:28.

3. See 1 Chronicles 12:32, 38.

Chapter One: What is an Armorbearer?

1. See 1 Samuel 16.

2. See Ephesians 6.

3. James Strong, *Strong's Complete Dictionary of Bible Words* (Thomas Nelson Publishers, 1996), **help** (#5375).

4. See 1 Timothy 1:18; 6:12.

5. See Exodus 17:11, 12.

6. See II Kings.

7. See I Samuel 16, 17.

8. Michael Agnes and Charlton Laird, eds., *Webster's New World Dictionary and Thesaurus*, Compilation Staff of Webster's New World Dictionary (Simon and Schuster, Inc., 1996), **serve,** p. 566.

9. Webster's, **refresh,** p. 520.

10. See Ecclesiastes 1:9, 10.

11. See 1 Samuel 16.

Chapter Two: Fulfilling Your High Calling to Ministry

1. Tommy Tenney, *God's Secrets to Greatness* (Ventura: Regal Books, 2000), p.48.

2. See 1 Corinthians 12:20, 22.

3. See I Kings 19:19-21.

4. See John 15:16.

5. See Revelation 17:14.

6. See 1 Corinthians 12:28.

7. John 15:16.

8. I Samuel 30:24.

9. See 1 Corinthians 12:27, 28.

10. See 1 Corinthians 12:18.

11. See Acts 6.

12. See 2 Peter 1:2-10.

13. See Romans 12:6,7 AMP

14. See Daniel 1:20.

15. See Ephesians 1:17.

16. Flegal KM, Carroll MD, Kuczmarski RJ, Johnson CL. *Overweight and Obesity in the United States: Prevalence and Trends,* 1960-1994. *Int J Obes.* 1998; 22:39-47.

17. See Romans 5:3, 4 (The Living Bible, Tyndale House Publishers, Inc., 1971).

18. See 1 Peter 1:14.

19. See Romans 12:10.

20. See 1 Peter 2:17.

21. See Ephesians 6:18.

22. See 1 John 3:18.

23. See 2 Timothy 2:21 (The Living Bible, Tyndale House Publishers, Inc., 1971).

24. See 2 Peter 1:2-10.

Chapter Three: Anointed to Serve

1. See Acts 6:1-6.

2. See John 14:15-21.

3. See James 3:13-17.

4. See Romans 11:29.

5. See Matthew 25:14-30.

6. See Revelation 3:15, 16.

7. See 1 Peter 1:16.

8. Kenneth E. Hagin, Sr., *I Believe in Visions* (Tulsa: RHEMA Bible Church, 1984), p. 57.

9. See 1 Corinthians 9:27.

10. See 1 Corinthians 13:1-13.

11. See Jeremiah 33:3.

Chapter Four: Choosing God's View of Servanthood

1. See Philippians 2:7.

2. See Ephesians 6:7.

3. See 1 Chronicles 9:17-33.

4. See 1 Chronicles 9:20

5. See 1 Chronicles 9:22.

6. See 1 Chronicles 9:23 TLB.

7. See 1 Chronicles 9:29 TLB.

8. See 1 Chronicles 9:33,34 TLB paraphrased.

9. See James 1:27.

10. See Hebrews 12:2.

11. See 1 Corinthians 10:31b

Chapter Five: Understanding the Flow of Authority

1. See Ephesians 6:12.

2. See Romans 13:2.

3. See Matthew 8:5-13.

4. Earma Broadway Brown, *Broken Church Recovery* (Dallas: Arrow Productions, 1997).

5. See Ephesians 5:20.

6. See Hebrews 13:17.

7. See 1 Peter 5:5a paraphrased.

8. See Acts 9:16 AMP

9. 1 Timothy 2:1, 2.

10. See Luke 2:41-52 paraphrased.

Chapter Six: Being the Gift of Support

1. See 1 Peter 4:10-11.

2. See Numbers 18:6.

3. See 1 Corinthians 12:18.

4. See 1 Peter 1:16.

5. See Luke 11:13 paraphrased.

6. See Exodus 4:14-17.

7. See Exodus 17:11-12.

8. See 1 Peter 4:13

9. See 1 Corinthians 12:12-21.

10. See Exodus 6:20; 7:1-2; 14; 17:1-7; 18; Deuteronomy 1:9-18; Leviticus 8-9; Exodus 17:8-16.

Chapter Seven: Developing the Spirit of Armorbearing

1. See Jeremiah 36; 43.

2. See 1 Corinthians 12:18.

3. 1 Peter 3:8.

4. John 15:13.

5. See Matthew 20:1-16.

6. John 9:4.

7. See John 15:13.

8. See Proverbs 18:12.

9. See 1 Thessalonians 5:12, 13.

10. See 2 Timothy 3:12.

11. See John 15:18a, 20a.

12. See John 15:19.

13. See Exodus 16:2; 86:9.

14. See Hebrews 6:1a.

15. See II Kings 3:11-27.

Chapter Nine: From the Heart of an Armorbearer

1. See Numbers 16-18.

2. See 1 Samuel 14.

3. See Exodus 17:11-12.

4. See John 15:16.

5. See Exodus 31:1, 6.

6. John C. Maxwell, *21 Irrefutable Laws of Leadership* (Nashville: Thomas Nelson Publishers, 1998), p. 90.

7. See 2 Corinthians 13:1.

8. See 1 Peter 5:5.

9. See John 15:20.

10. See Psalms 62:1, 2.

11. See John 15:13.

12. T.D. Jakes, *Keepers of the Flame,* 4-tape audio series, tape 4 (Dallas: T.D. Jakes Ministries, 2000).

13. See Mark 14:38.

14. See 1 Samuel 14.

Chapter Ten: The Ministry of an Armorbearer

1. See Matthew 10:41

2. See Exodus 31:1-11; Hebrews 8:2.

3. See 1 Timothy 2:2

4. See 1 Chronicles 12:1-40.

5. See Judges 7:8.

6. See John 9:4.

7. Matthew 25:45-51

8. 1 Corinthian 13.

9. 1 Chronicles 12.

Chapter Eleven: Developing the Character of Christ

1. See Deuteronomy 8:4.

2. See Hebrews 12:11.

3.   See Deuteronomy 8:2, 3.

4.   See Romans 5:4, 5.

5.   John Maxwell, *The 21 Indispensable Qualities of a Leader* (Nashville: Thomas Nelson Publishers, 1999), p. 4.

6.   See I Samuel 3.

7.   See 1 Chronicles 12:22.

8.   See 2 Timothy 2:3.

9.   See 1 John 1:9, Romans 8:28

Chapter Twelve: Being an Anticipator

1.   See James 1:5.

2.   See Isaiah 65:24a.

3.   See John 12:1-8.

4.   See Matthew 10:39.

5.   See Matthew 7:14.

6.   See Psalms 33:1.

7.   See Proverbs 22:3; 27:12.

Chapter Thirteen: The Gehazi Factor

1.   See 1 Corinthians 10:6.

2.   See 2 Kings 5:20-27.

3.   See 1 Peter 5:6.

4.   See Galatians 5:16-26.

5. See 1 Peter 5:8

Chapter Fourteen: Daring to Be Faithful

1. See Romans 5:20.

2. Buddy Bell, *The Ministry of Helps Handbook* (Tulsa, OK: Harrison House, Inc., 1990), p. 20.

3. See Genesis 18:19 TLB; James 2:21-26; 5:17 TLB paraphrased.

4. Hebrews 6:10.

5. See Romans 12:1.

6. See Hebrews 12:11.

7. See Psalms 91:4.

8. See 1 Corinthians 4:1, 2.

9. See Matthew 18:19.

10. See Joshua 24.

11. See John 18:15-27; 21:15-23.

ABOUT THE AUTHOR

Earma B. Brown and her husband Varn began preaching and teaching the Word of God in a local jail and prison ministry. She says the weekly Bible studies, services, and bi-monthly dormitory cell sessions changed their lives and gave them a strong foundation in ministry.

After more than seven years, she and her husband sensed a call to devote a greater focus to their local church ministries. They have served in many different capacities as Helps ministers for more than 15 years.

Through those experiences, God gave them a special compassion and understanding for His armorbearers and ministers of helps.

They have been married for over ten years and reside in Carrollton, Texas, a Dallas suburb. Earma and Varn now serve as a part of their local church's small group ministry leadership as well as leading a team to feed and clothe the poor in their city.

Earma believes the call on her life is to strengthen the Body of Christ and reach for the lost sheep in the Church. She says, "God called me to write for Him saying, 'Go now, write it down for them, and publish it in a book that for the days to come, it may be an ever-lasting witness.'" She has written and taught over five Bible class curriculums in her local church's Ministry of Education program. Her teaching and writing ministry includes topics designed for the helps ministry, new converts, small group study and women's ministry.

To contact the author write:

Earma Broadway Brown
P. O. Box 700641
Dallas, Texas 75370

Internet Address:
www.armorbearers.net

Please include your testimony or help received from this book when you write. Your prayer requests are welcome.

BIBLIOGRAPHY

Bell, Buddy. *The Ministry of Helps Handbook—How to be Totally Effective Serving in the Ministry of Helps.* Tulsa, OK: Harrison House, Inc., 1990.

Cape, David and Tenney, Tommy. *God's Secret to Greatness—The Power of the Towel.* Ventura, CA: Regal Books, 2000.

Eckhardt, John. *The Ministry Anointing of Helps.* Chicago, IL: Crusaders Ministries, 1991.

Grein, Janny. *Called Appointed Anointed—Prepare Your Life to be a Vessel for the Anointing and Glory of God.* Tulsa, OK: Harrison House, Inc., 1981.

Hagin, Kenneth E. *I Believe in Visions.* Tulsa, OK: Kenneth Hagin Ministries, Inc., 1984.

Jakes, T.D. *Keepers of the Flame—four Tape Audio Series.* Dallas, TX: T. D. Jakes Ministries, 2000.

Maxwell, John. *The 21 Irrefutable Laws of Leadership.* Nashville, TN: Thomas Nelson, Inc., 1991.

Nance, Terry. *God's Armorbearer—How to Serve God's Leaders.* Tulsa, OK: Harrison House Inc., 1990.

Nance, Terry. *God's Armorbearer II—How to Bloom Where God has Planted You.* Tulsa, OK: Harrison House Inc., 1994.

0-595-25095-5

Printed in the United States
17445LVS00005B/353